Just Unfriend Me …

Han Govern

John 14:27

Just Unfriend Me ... Or Not

A compilation of original posts on Facebook

Stan Parris

Pard
PUBLISHING

Pard Publishing
pardpubs@gmail.com

To contact the author directly, please email him at reddie2write@gmail.com.

ISBN: 978-1-7378477-2-4

Editor: Dennis A. Byrd
Cover illustration: Muhammad Ali Malik
          Alidesigns00 (Fiverr profile)
Author photo: Charlotte Parris
Book design: H. K. Stewart

Pard
PUBLISHING

Printed in the United States of America

To our children, **Kyle**, **Kelly**, and **Kenneth**.

Thanks for allowing me to not be too serious.

Contents

Foreword

When I began taking notice of the writing ability of Stan Parris, I probably was at least three-deep into his "Walmart Words" postings on Facebook. That's when I knew it wasn't a fluke or a lucky happenstance that made his postings both funny and readable. He definitely has a way with words, I thought, as I read the newest installment.

A short time later some close friends in Arkadelphia let us know that Stan, my longtime friend from Henderson State University days, was preaching the next Sunday at their little Southern Baptist church just a few short miles from where all of us—David and Judi Jenkins, frequent dinner friends Bobby and Judy Jones, Stan and Charlotte, and my wife, Linda, and I all finished our undergraduate degrees.

"We'll meet you at your house and ride out with you," we told Judi Jenkins, adding arrangements to attend the Sunday School class she was teaching from the same literature I was using in my class at First Baptist Church of Benton. I arranged for somebody to fill in for me and off we went. It wasn't the first time I'd heard Stan preach. We had attended services he led in two Benton churches while he was on furlough from the mission field in Venezuela, and we'd found our way to a tiny mission church in Southwest Little Rock that was part of the Immanuel Baptist Church family when Stan was missions pastor there. We had heard he was preaching the 11:00 a.m. service at the small church, so we arrived early enough to say hi and make lunch arrangements for afterward.

But, that Sunday at Cedar Grove Baptist Church—June 30, 2019—was special in many ways. The sermon reminded us of how we, as Christians, had become complacent in our spiritual lives. One line he delivered that Sunday related to the standard mantra that we are all sinners, then he added this gem: "Christians sin for one reason; we want to." Ouch.

Just before the service, there was some talk about how much we all were enjoying his musings about his shopping experiences at Walmart. I joined the many who had commented on his Facebook page by saying he should write a book. He said he was working on something and I responded that I would be happy to help. "I may take you up on that," he said, just before wandering up to his front row seat to park next to his granddaughter, Sara, who often accompanied him on his post-retirement Sunday morning trips to churches near and far to bring a Sunday morning message.

Not long after that Sunday, Stan and I began to talk about his writings on the phone and via text message. He laid out his plan to put together several mission stories from his time in Maricaibo, Venezuela, and in many other countries, including Turkey and China, as a missions pastor. He had kept notes, he explained, on little pocket-sized notebooks, during these many trips. He started pulling those out of storage and would write about the experiences. He often has repeated that translating from those notes "put him back" in the places he'd served, enabling him to recreate the sights and sounds, and even the smells, in his head as he wrote.

A few months later, Stan's first book, *Just Outside of Hope*, was born and I was privileged to play a very small part in that publication. Stan gave me the freedom to edit his writings and allowed me to write the Foreword to that book. After doing considerable research, we formed our own publishing partnership, and worked with a very capable and experienced H. K. Stewart to put all of what Stan had written into book form.

Now, Stan comes back to his writing roots by publishing his Facebook postings about shopping at Walmart and other postings, which became known as his "Just Saying" posts. It again was my privilege to be a very small part of this new book. But, more importantly, it has been rewarding in many ways to come full circle in my friendship with Stan. After many years—and I do mean many—Stan and I have developed an even deeper friendship through his writings. It is my hope it provides as much enjoyment to you as it has to me.

Dennis Byrd
August 2023

Introduction

When I retired from fulltime ministry in November of 2016, I told my wife I would like to take on the responsibility of grocery shopping. I also told her I would start cooking breakfast for us every morning.

Cooking breakfast turned out to be the easier of the two.

I had gone shopping with her for years, mainly to do the heavy lifting, the reaching for items on the top shelf, and the unloading of the groceries into and out of our truck. My first solo trip to Walmart was a life-changer in that it motivated me to sit down and write some of my shopping frustrations. Each trip to Walmart provided another interesting experience, and those weekly writings became kind of popular as I posted them on Facebook under the title, "Walmart Words." The first 37 chapters of this book, with minor edits, were posted consecutively on Facebook from March 1, 2019, to February 20, 2020.

As my friends read those posts, they most definitely identified with my shopping frustrations and observations, and they also encouraged me to keep writing. So, I did. Some of my friends suggested that I needed to compile these writings into a book. After writing about my shopping experiences for almost a year, I had a desire to write about other experiences … life experiences.

Honestly, I became a little concerned when friends began calling me "The Walmart Man" or "Walmart Stan." One of my friends wrote, "Sure miss your preaching, but I love your Walmart stories."

I began to ask myself if I really wanted Walmart stories to be my legacy. The final straw occurred one Sunday morning as I was preaching in a small, nearby church. An elderly lady walked down the center aisle during the closing hymn to tell me that she had to leave a little early, but she did not want to leave without telling me how much she enjoyed my Walmart stories. She did not even mention the sermon I had just preached.

So, I began to write and share on Facebook about everyday kinds of things, things that we all see and experience, but never take the time to fully contemplate. I called those writings, "Just Saying," and my friends strongly suggested that I also include those writings in a book. So, I did. Most of those writings were during the lock-down months of Covid 19, a time when we all had plenty of time on our hands.

This book contains most of my first attempts at being a writer. Even though I pastored churches, served as a missionary, and wrote and preached hundreds and hundreds of sermons, this kind of writing is different. There is no Biblical passage to use as a launching pad; there is no outline to follow as you explain and attempt to make application, but there is inspiration. I have sensed the same presence of God as I have attempted to put thoughts into words and to paint clear word pictures. I am not stating that I am a gifted writer, but that writing is one of God's gifts to me. I write, not because I am good at it, but because it gives me great joy. I hope that you enjoy the observations and life-lessons of this book.

Book One

Walmart Words

Chapter 1

Enter or Exit

Dear Walmart,

I am a loyal customer, so there are a few things that I would like to get off my mind. I know you cannot do anything about my two major complaints: customers who enter through the exit door, and those who take the 45-degree stroll across the pedestrian walkway (please just take the quickest straight-line route and then "45-degree it" to your vehicle).

However, there are some things that would increase our "shopping pleasure" (oxymoron of the year). Please consider not stocking your shelves during the busiest shopping hours. I mean, really. It is congested enough with the shoppers, the conversations, the cell phone texters, the family reunions, the class reunions, and the health updates, but when your own employees are asked to climb their large ladders which completely block the already too-narrow aisles … well, you get the picture. Would it be possible to take care of the shelf stocking at a time other than 11 a.m. to 1 p.m. on a Friday? I would be glad to come very early one morning and stock for an hour or two. You don't even have to pay me. I'll do it for one of your rotisserie chickens; I mean, heck, I'm almost 73 years old and retired, I'm up at all hours of the night, and I only live 1.3 miles from your chicken … I mean your store. I promise you that if you gave me this opportunity, I would put the merchandise back in the same place week after week after week instead of making your customers play scavenger hunt every time they enter through the exit door.

Sincerely,
An observant shopper

P.S. I wasn't going to mention this, but one of your stockers gave me an "attitude look" today when I mentioned to him that we were log-jammed on aisle 10. If I were not such a nice guy, I might have been offended and pulled him off the ladder and anointed him with your Great Value Canola.

Chapter 2

Added Shopping Features

In recent months, I have become the primary grocery shopper at our house. It has been a learning process. I have yet to complete the perfect shopping list. My goal is to, one day, make it home without having to use a lifeline (call Charlotte for clarification), without asking for assistance in finding an item, and purchasing exactly the items on my list, including right size, right brand, right number, and right carb count. So far, I've come very close but have fallen short.

I have purchased zucchini thinking they were cucumbers. I have been amazed at all you can do to a tomato … paste, sauce, diced, petites, roasted, crushed … to say nothing of the different brands and can sizes. I have yet to be able to find minced garlic without assistance … did I mention that our local store often rearranges everything?

I've already ranted about some of the shopping challenges at our local Walmart, but for the most part, I enjoy my frequent trips. I enjoy seeing local friends and neighbors and the added intrigue of seeing people who appear to be visiting our planet. Who are these people and where do they come from?

Our Walmart has added features. We are a college town, which means the addition of 3,000 shoppers and we are very close to a nice lake and recreational area, which means more shoppers. We also have a lot of deer hunters in our part of the world, which I really like because it makes for friendly conversation. "Get your deer yet?" is the most repeated phrase in our Walmart during the winter months, especially around the crackers, cheese, and summer sausage aisles.

The college students bring an additional challenge. It is one of those interesting facts about life that the very things 20-year-olds eat to maintain a healthy lifestyle are the very things I need just to stay alive. I thought college students lived on chips and Ramen noodles, but in our Walmart, they rush for the fresh fruit, fresh salads, and my life sustaining cereal, Honey Nut Cheerios. I don't know why they seem to prefer my cereal, but everyone my age understands why it has become a necessity for me.

It never fails that I come home from Walmart with a good story or a humbling, eye-opening experience. Recently, my eyes have been opened about the aging process. I am beginning to feel old and despite my attempts at denial, I look old. I knew I had reached a new level of aging on my most recent Walmart trip. As I walked in the door, I saw a friend I had not seen in a long time. Normally, I hear greetings like, "You're looking good," or maybe, "You're taking good care of yourself," or "You're holding up well." My friend's greeting was a first for me: "You're walking good," he said. Really? That's supposed to make me feel good? Since then, all I can think about is that one day, I won't be able to walk to aisle 5 to beat the young folks to the cereal.

Chapter 3

Just 1.3 Miles to Walmart

"We're only 1.3 miles from Walmart." This is a statement that can be heard often at our house. Especially when I return home without perfectly completing the grocery list, or just after unloading the groceries when we realize that we are completely out of trash bags or fruit snacks or tuna (in oil not water) or something that we forgot to put on the list. So, instead of sinking into depression or frustration, and instead of admitting yet another shopping failure, it's so convenient to just utter those important words, "Well, hey, we're just 1.3 miles from Walmart."

On one Sunday morning, my then-12-year-old granddaughter and I were headed to a church where I was scheduled to preach. We were driving through some pretty small communities in the rural area of Southwest Arkansas when she said, "Papa, where do these people go to school and where do they shop? I mean, it's not like there's a Walmart close by."

That was my cue. "Yeah, they can't say it's only 1.3 miles from Walmart." Can you picture her middle school eye roll? She has heard that family mantra more than a few times.

This led to a conversation about Long's Grocery Store located at the intersection of the Old Washington Highway and Melrose Lane about three miles north of Hope, Arkansas. That's where I grew up a long time ago before Walmart existed. I told her about my parents often sending me on the 100-yard trip on my bicycle to "get milk and bread." My mom always bought groceries in town on Friday afternoon when she got paid, but we were always running out of something. So, I would ride my bike down the red dirt road, pick up the milk and bread, and ask Mrs. Long to "charge it." She would write it down on a small tablet (each family on Melrose Lane had their own tablet), and then she would place the Borden milk in one small brown paper bag and the short loaf of Holsom bread in another. There is a real art to crumpling and wrapping the top of a paper bag around a handlebar grip and riding your bicycle without wrecking or smashing the bread. I was a master at this.

We arrived at the church before I had time to tell her about other great stories that center around that little store. It was a Gulf "filling station" as well as a grocery store. It was also a kind of gathering place for older men who loved to talk about fox hunting. Mrs. Long was always behind the wooden counter, but most of the time Mr. Long would be sitting with the men in the small circle of chairs just behind the Coke box. I can still visualize that store and I can remember standing in front of the candy counter peering through the glass wondering what Mother would do if I bought a Payday and asked Mrs. Long to put it on the tab. I digress.

Anyway, my granddaughter and I had a wonderful Sunday together and when we got home, she went to the refrigerator and announced that we were out of milk. No problem! It's just 1.3 miles to Walmart.

Chapter 4

Miss Those Greeters

In my opinion, one of the most interesting and inviting things about Walmart was the greeters. There was just something warm and encouraging about walking through the door and being greeted with a smile and a face-to-face "Welcome to Walmart."

I am not a fan of the greetings being shouted out from the back of some noisy stores with music blasting and no eye contact from an employee, who, in reality, has no idea who just walked through the door. The door opens, triggering a bell, and it could be an armed, masked robber walking into the store, and the same insincere, "Welcome to ——" would be shouted across the room. I prefer the smiling, friendly, personal "Welcome" of the Walmart greeters. They have disappeared—some sort of cost-cutting measure, I guess. I miss them.

Recently, I have noticed the greeters have been replaced by employees seated just inside the store, who appear to be observing customers as they enter and exit the store. I'm not sure about their purpose, but I'm hoping they are doing a study and gathering information about switching the Enter and Exit doors. We don't live in England, and we have been trained to stay to the right. I know we can see the well-placed Enter and Exit signs to our left, but muscle memory causes us to hesitate for just a step or two as we ultimately obey the Walmart rules. So, we enter the store feeling either guilty about having disobeyed the signs or feeling perplexed about that brief moment of uncertainty when we followed the rules, but don't feel right about it. That's where the all-important greeters come in. "Welcome to Walmart," says the smiling, friendly, gray-haired person, and my guilt or my insecurity is gone. Now I'm ready to spend an hour and a half pushing a wobbly wheel buggy down a narrow, crowded aisle looking for items that have been replaced or moved to a different part of the store.

Maybe instead of greeters on the inside of the store, they should provide counselors just outside the door. But should they be on the right or the left?

Chapter 5

No Uneventful Trips

A few weeks ago, I came home after a frustrating shopping experience at our local Walmart. Within a few minutes I had written a "Dear Walmart note" that was a kind of comic relief therapy. It was intended to be a lighthearted description of an average grocery shopping experience, and it seemed to resonate with the experience of other shoppers.

On my next trip to Walmart, it dawned on me that, for me, there is no such thing as an uneventful trip to Walmart. Never. It might be a conversation, an observation, or a frustration, but I always arrive home with a story. Always.

While traveling in China several years ago, my host told me that their city had a Walmart—a most unusual Walmart. It was built underground; in fact, it was built underneath a very nice city park. At that very moment we were walking on top of this Chinese Walmart. Hold that thought.

A very interesting thing about China is the existence of what some refer to as "English Corners." These are different locations in a city where young Chinese students gather to practice speaking English. It might be on a street corner, in a tea house, or in someone's apartment. Native English speakers are a rarity at these groups, but always welcome because there are not many opportunities to practice with a real English speaker. Another interesting fact is that many times the English student will choose his or her own English name. It might be a real name, like Mark or Angie, or it might be a name that we would not consider to be a normal name. I met a young man at one English Corner who introduced himself: "Hello, my name is Human Skeleton." He obviously was in the early stages of his language learning, so my host said to him in very slow, clear English, "You must change your name."

So, we are headed down this long escalator to experience shopping at a Walmart in China. About halfway down I spotted him standing at the bottom waiting for us to step off the escalator. That's right, your friendly Walmart greeter. A young Chinese man sporting a blue Walmart vest and his Walmart name tag. He smiled and said, (use your best non-English speaker accent) "Welcome to Walmart." I smiled back, but my eyes went immediately to his name tag ... Jesus Christ.

I made attempts at trying to quiz him about his chosen English name, but his only response was, "Welcome to Walmart," which are three more words than I can say in Chinese. I will refrain from sharing everything that went through my mind and heart at that moment. I really wanted to talk to that young man about His Name, but my reason for sharing this story is to give more evidence that there is no such thing as an uneventful trip to Walmart. Never.

Chapter 6

No Lifeline Required

A relatively easy grocery run today—parking spot next to the cart return, shopping cart with four working wheels, and aisles not crowded with shoppers. I was able to complete the list without using a lifeline, and made only one error with my tie-breaker strategy of larger is always better. I forgot that it does have to fit on the pantry shelf or in the refrigerator. One major stumble came in the sandwich bag area. I did spend more than the usual amount of time deciding between Ziplock or Hefty, slide or easy seal, storage or freezer, and 90 or 135 count. I have learned it is better not to say, "Does it really matter?" I still get frustrated with so many options.

We were living in Venezuela during the 1980s; it was a wonderful place then. Unlike the situation there today, there was plenty of food on the shelves, but not many options. There were only two or three types of cereal from which to choose, two brands of toothpaste, a good supply, but very limited options. A missionary returning to the States experiences reverse culture shock trying to decide among so many products. Inexperienced shoppers can also find themselves standing, staring, confused … I call it shopping shelf shock. It can be traumatic. I was almost there, but made a quick decision that was influenced by my dad's motto (Get it and let's go) and, well, let's just say we now have a nice supply of sandwich bags.

I breezed through the rest of the list and found an open checkout lane with a smiling checker. Really. I'm serious. She smiled and said, "Y'all sure use a lot of sandwich bags." Not really. I just made that up. What she really said caught me by surprise. She said, "You look like the guy in the movie I just watched."

"Really," I said, thinking to myself, *I can't wait to get home and tell Charlotte about this.* "Yeah, it was a horror movie, and this guy was a priest and he had a cross around his neck and he was casting a demon out of this girl." It's almost impossible to have a serious conversation in a checkout line, but I did say to her that I was surprised that she would watch a movie like that. She replied, "Oh, that stuff is not real." I told her that as a missionary in South America I had personally seen demon possession and demonic influences, and it is very much real. The impatient shopper behind me resulted in cutting our conversation short, but I pray that there will be further conversations with this young woman. By the way, I hope you know that is very much real.

Chapter 7

An Amateur (and a Pro)

I am a very inexperienced shopper. I'm learning, but I am an amateur. This morning Charlotte felt like making the trip with me to Walmart and I was excited. I would finally get a chance to "show off" my improved shopping skills, and I could finally prove to her that, like I've been telling her for months, they no longer carry some of her favorite products. Much like a basketball team that controls the tempo of a game, after only a few seconds in the store, it was obvious that I was not in control.

She paid no attention to my well-thought-out list. I always have a list and I compile my list in the order in which I place the items in the cart. Who doesn't do that? Paper goods first on my way to the back of the store to get the butter, eggs, milk, right turn to drinks, left turn to cereal, then chips, etc. I work my way from aisle to aisle checking off each item from my neatly organized list.

Charlotte did not even have a list, and we meandered through unfamiliar parts of the store. She seemed to know exactly what she wanted and where it was located. She could spot the item from 25 feet away and pick up speed as she closed in on it. I was confused about where to place these new items in the cart. Dog treats, toothpicks, alcohol (not the drinking kind), scented candles, a ceramic skillet … none of those things had ever been on my list (who in the world is this pioneer woman?).

We finally made it to my familiar aisles, but things did not improve. Items that I have not been able to find for months seem to just appear in plain sight. I was losing all credibility as she walked quickly from item to item without even slowing down to hunt. There was no hunting. There were no long pauses. Those items saw her coming and just scooted to the edge and leaned forward.

She even found the vegetable straws. How was I to know they would be found in "snacks" and not in "chips." Weeks earlier I had easily found the vegetable puffs on the chip aisle. I mean what's the difference between snacks and chips? Who makes those decisions? It's confusing for an amateur, but Charlotte was not confused and snatched them off the shelf without breaking stride.

I know she smirked. I didn't actually see it, but I know she did. After check-out, I was in a trance-like state as I pushed the cart to the truck. I had been "schooled" and we both knew it. I am such an amateur.

Chapter 8

Just Being Observant

In case you're wondering, I did not plan to continue writing these thoughts, but the ideas just keep coming. Also, I have been amazed at how many of you can identify with some of these observations and your comments are encouraging.

Obviously, I am a supporter of Walmart. Since retiring I spend more time there than I spend in church. In fact, I spend more time in Walmart than anywhere other than at home. Yes, I realize how sad that is. There are other shopping options in our town; actually, there is one other option, but it is three stoplights away. Also, where else but Walmart can you walk around with a cart containing groceries, bird seed, Dr. Scholl's socks, pajamas, shotgun shells, a vacuum cleaner, rat poison, and a lawn mower tire without anyone even looking at you funny? Plus, you can make all these purchases while you're having the oil changed in your car. So, any comments I make about Walmart are just my random observations.

I am very observant, but in a weird sort of way. My closest friends know that I am a counter. I count things. Yes, I count things like ceiling tiles, cows in a pasture, the number of cowboys in posse, the number of steps to the mailbox, and the number of feet in a Walmart aisle. Our local Walmart aisles are 6 ½-feet wide. The shopping carts we use to maneuver these aisles are 2 feet wide. So, if we pay attention to our maneuvering and hug the outside of the aisle, we can meet and pass each other with a 2 feet 3-inch safety space. But if we cheat to the middle of the aisle or park said cart in the middle of said aisle, we disrupt the flow of said maneuvering. Also, and this is just an observation, if we bend down to reach an item on the bottom shelf and extend our bottom out into the middle of the narrow aisle, not only have we stopped the flow of said maneuvering, but we have also made those "behind" us extremely uncomfortable. That is especially so if our "behind" is wider than a shopping cart. In those moments I am glad that I count ceiling tiles.

One other interesting observation: In our local Walmart there is one aisle that is one foot wider than the other aisles. I am not making this up; the candy aisle is wider. Just an observation.

So, Walmart shoppers, the lesson today is, "Hug those aisles and count those tiles."

Chapter 9

Waiting on "Flat Squirrel"

I promise that when I stop observing these things, I will stop documenting these thoughts, but my eyes just won't stop watching and my mind just won't stop wondering. I recently saw a quote that accurately describes many Walmart shoppers: "The world is full of flat squirrels who could not make up their mind."

I totally understand that grocery shopping is work, especially if there are dietary concerns because of health issues. For many of us, reading the labels for carb count and calories is just part of the experience; but if you are standing in front of the bacon selections, you are probably not counting carbs so why does it take so long to choose a package of bacon.

On a recent shopping adventure, I stood and waited on a lady to make her bacon decision. Other shoppers grew tired of waiting and moved on down the aisle to Jimmy Dean sausage and Earl Campbell Hot Links, but not me. I was intrigued with this lady, who was obviously on a mission.

She shuffled through package after package of bacon looking at the front and back of each package and returning each one to the stack. I was determined to stand there watching and waiting. I'm retired so I had until 3 p.m.—that's when *The Andy Griffith Show* comes on. I guessed her to be in her mid-sixties and she had her pre-school grandson sitting in the buggy. While "Flat Squirrel" was running back and forth between bacon packages, I was playing peek-a-boo with "Baby Squirrel." She never knew. She never looked over her shoulder to check on him, and he never whimpered or seemed anxious. I assumed that he was used to this, so I stood watching and waiting … I am not making this up … for eight minutes. The frozen chicken tenders in my buggy were beginning to thaw.

I had several thoughts running through my mind like, "I know you're looking for the package with the most meat and the less fat, but you're going to fry it so it's going to kill you anyway. Just choose your poison and move on to the pork chops." For eight minutes I stood there. In his heyday, Roger Bannister could have already run two miles.

My mind does crazy things at times, and this was one of those times. I begin to think about the children of Israel. I've read that there could have been as many as two million Hebrews who were part of the Exodus out of Egypt. If each one took eight minutes to choose a portion of pork, no wonder the Lord would not permit them to eat it. By the way, follow that line of thinking and you will see that it would take 30 years for two million to finally make a choice. Add ten years for that many people to check out and there you have it—40 years in the wilderness. I know … weird, right?

Anyway, "Flat Squirrel" finally made her choice and crossed over into the promise land. I just grabbed the package on top and headed for the Jordan.

Chapter 10

The Language of Flowers

When you are learning a second language, one of the challenges is learning the vocabulary for different situations. For example, when I went to get my haircut for the first time in Venezuela, I had no idea how to explain exactly how I wanted him to cut it. I bluffed my way through it and came home looking like Porter Wagoner. Every situation has its own vocabulary.

Today, I went to the Garden Center of our local Walmart. I don't speak Garden. I know nothing about planting a garden or working in a flower bed. My wife, however, is fluent in many, many languages. She loves flowers and garden stuff. Every year we buy stuff, and she tells me where to dig, how deep to dig, and what to put in the holes I just dug. So today, Walmart had just received a new supply of flowers, shrubs, and stuff. Big, tall trays of stuff. We walked through the aisles, and she knew the name of each and every flower. It was like she was speaking in tongues. Names of flowers just flew out of her mouth. Names like Foxglove, which by the way, is good for the heart, unless you get too much and it will kill you. I was not amused that my wife had that kind of information stored away in her memory. I responded that there should be a warning label somewhere about that. I even tried to make a joke. "How many gloves can a fox wear?" I said. Without saying a word, she put one in the cart.

We moved on through five kinds of Salvia, Dragon Wing Begonias (if a fox glove will kill you, why do you also need a dragon wing?), Coleus, Lobelia, Lantana, and Lily. I knew that one because every Easter the church would be full of them and they made my sinuses run and drip on my sermon notes.

One good thing about the Garden Center is they have their own check-out area. That's so your perennials and your annuals don't get put into the same bags with your hummus, or is it humus … I don't eat either one. Charlotte left me by myself to check out. She said she was going to look for a philodendron. I panicked because I thought that must be in the Pharmacy area and that was too far away to hear me calling for help. I did buy some time when the lady in front of me, who obviously did not understand the rules about Garden Center check out, placed (I am not making this up) $147 of groceries on the counter and one bag of fire ant killer.

Finally, it was my turn, and the checker was understandably not in a great mood. "How many Salvia do you have?" she asked. Long pause. She recognized immediately that I was as lost as a gringo in a Venezuelan barber shop. She was kind and asked me to hand her the red ones first.

Charlotte finally returned and I asked her if philodendron was good for a headache. I must learn to speak more languages.

Chapter 11

Family (and Other) Reactions

Thanks to all of you for your comments and encouraging words about these Walmart Words. I'm not sure how many more "reports" I'll be sharing, but it sure has been interesting.

There have been a few negative results of posting my observations. For example, my children and especially my grandchildren do not find my posts funny. When I ask them if they have read the latest post, all I get is a "yeah," combined with an obvious eye roll. They will not even smile in my presence. Our 12-year-old, who would jump in my truck for a trip to Walmart a few weeks ago, will not even come out of the back room. Our oldest son complains that he cannot go anywhere in town without being asked about his dad's Walmart stories. The real clincher was when he traveled out of state to visit friends from college days and they greeted him with, "Hey, we love your dad's Walmart stories." My family is embarrassed. Charlotte is very supportive, but I think she laughs at my stories because she needs me to continue doing the shopping.

There have been reports of Walmart shoppers in other communities showing up with tape measures in the candy aisles, stop watches in the bacon section, and long lines at the deli, requesting the rotisserie chicken. When I arrived at the Walmart parking lot a few days ago, a lady I know asked if she could put her groceries in the car and follow me around. Others respond by avoiding me completely for fear of being mentioned in a post. One of my friends in another city reported that she entered through the exit door, and felt so guilty that she turned around, went back outside, and entered through the correct door. Those shoppers watching her erratic behaviors were frozen in confusion. "Flat Squirrel" reports are coming in from as far away as Florida.

Many of you have asked if I have heard from anyone in the Walmart corporate office. I have. I did not know that Walmart had company counselors and that they offered free counseling. Also, many are concerned that I must be bored in my retirement. This is not true. When I'm not at Walmart, I am very busy unloading groceries from my truck, putting groceries in the pantry, counting the number of Walmart bags we have hanging on the wall, and making the shopping list of things I forgot, things I could not find, or things that I know they have hidden in the back but won't tell me. No, really, I'm enjoying retirement.

I've always dreamed of dodging electric carts, standing in long lines, opening eight cartons of eggs before finding one without cracked eggs, squeezing between two oversized ladies who are blocking the frozen vegetables, trying to impress people by picking up and smelling fruit, (I have no idea why I'm doing this), figuring out how to get a pineapple into a cheap plastic bag, and looking at bottles of spices until I'm cross-eyed trying to find saffron. I don't care what you say, they are not in alphabetical order.

Many of you have asked if I'm going to write a book. Honestly, I don't have the time.

Note: Some of you seemed to be concerned that I may have betrayed my calling and lost my passion for ministry. You can rest easy. I never walk into Walmart spiritually unprepared. In fact, if you are not right with God, you will not survive in there.

Chapter 12

Parking Lot Traffic

When our family arrived in Venezuela 35 years ago, one of the greatest adjustments was surviving in Venezuelan traffic. There are no words to paint the picture. Stop signs were non-existent, traffic lights were only suggestions, brakes were seldom used, but horns were an absolute necessity. As you approached an intersection, you never made eye contact with oncoming drivers; you just focused on their front bumper. When that front bumper dipped, you knew that the driver had just touched his brake pedal and you had just won the right of way.

As I traveled to other countries, I found each culture had similar "traffic rules for survival." A taxi driver in Pakistan told me, "He who runs first wins." I asked a driver in Turkey if there was a reason why they drove so fast. He smiled as he said, "We drive like our Ottoman ancestors rode their horses." Chinese taxi drivers drive like they will be placed in labor camps if anyone passes them.

But honestly, I feel safer in the traffic of any of those countries than I feel in a Walmart parking lot. The next time you make a statement like, "I'm going to run to Walmart and get a few things," think about the signals you have just sent to your brain (for non-Arkansans: we really don't mean that we are going to "run." We mean that we are having to go somewhere we really don't want to go, so we are going to do it as quickly as possible while gritting our teeth because nobody else in the family will do it, so we are going to jump in the car and drive like an Ottoman Turk riding his horse into battle, so stay out of our way).

Instead, try saying this: "I'm going to Walmart and I do not have to be in a hurry. They have plenty of milk hidden in the back. I am going to obey all speed limits and all traffic laws. I WILL use my blinker. I will turn into the parking lot with all four wheels touching the pavement. I am aware that there are at least 200 places to park, and I do not have to race anyone for the one spot closest to the entrance. If there are painted arrows on the pavement, I will not drive down an aisle if those arrows are pointing at me. I will not disobey that arrow and back my car into an empty parking spot. When I find an available parking space, I will make sure that my vehicle remains within the white lines designating that specific parking space. I will not pull my vehicle three feet across the line into the space in front of me.

"When I have completed my shopping, placed my groceries in the vehicle, put on my seat belt, and started the engine, I will not sit there FOREVER checking my phone, listening to messages, or checking my make up. I will never, never, ever stop my vehicle in the pedestrian crossing lane, get out of my vehicle and unload my groceries from the shopping cart into my vehicle. Upon exiting the parking space, I will not take off like a crazy person at a 45-degree angle toward the exits. I am not the only person living (and driving) on this planet. I do not live in Venezuela or Pakistan or Turkey or China; I live in America where people are kind, considerate, courteous, selfless, and patient."

Yeah, right. On second thought, I will get in the car and "run to Walmart." I will not make eye contact. Warning to everyone: "Stay out of my way!"

Chapter 13

Rude Shopper on the Move

Let's talk about Friendliness. Niceness. Courtesy. Remember those qualities? My dad was one of the friendliest people I have ever known. He would speak to everyone, wave to everyone, and smile when he greeted everyone. I am not making this up or creating a nostalgic, wishful memory. If you knew my dad, you know this to be true.

As I walked through the Walmart aisles today, it occurred to me, that were my dad walking with me, he would probably be disappointed and confused. It's not just that we no longer speak to one another, we won't even make eye contact. In addition to serious unfriendliness, we can be rather rude, and I witnessed a few examples of rudeness today.

You've probably seen the same "I'm headed to the back of the store with this buggy without making any stops or taking my eyes off the back wall" shopper. This rude shopper sped past me, dodging the lady in the electric cart, and barely missing the guy who had just asked me where to find saltine crackers (I actually knew their exact location). Determination was written on his wrinkled forehead and on his white-knuckled grip on the cart handle. "Rude shopper" was moving fast, and Lord help the person who stepped in front of the cart. Cart rage flooded my body. I wanted revenge. Even my dad would not be nice to this person. Thoughts of confrontation began to take shape in my mind. I reminded myself that I was a Christian, but surely there was room for righteous indignation. I watched "Rude Shopper" move someone's cart out of the way to reach the green beans. No words of apology or "excuse me." Not once did this person stop at the end of an aisle to yield to oncoming traffic. "Rude Shopper" was quickly around the corner and out of sight, but not out of mind. There should be penalties for rudeness, and shoppers should be allowed to make "citizens arrests."

Seriously, if Walmart is not going to have greeters, why not have flaggers? They could place (or throw) a red flag on the cart of any shopper caught in rude behavior. When arriving at checkout, if a cart has more than three red flags, that shopper is required to go directly to the sale rack in the clothing department and find at least three articles of clothing that are on the correct size hangers. They'll be there until their ice cream melts. I would gladly volunteer to be a flagger. I would have loved to have "thrown the flag" at "Rude Shopper's" head … I mean cart. If greeters made us feel more welcomed, flaggers would make us all smile more … like my dad.

Chapter 14

Papa with Good Taste

Charlotte and I have five grandchildren, four granddaughters and one grandson. If you are a grandparent, you know how you cherish time spent with grandchildren. We have been blessed in that we have lived in the same city as our three oldest for most of their lives. So, hopefully, you will not think it to be extremely unusual that I have become a shopping partner with our, then-12-year-old granddaughter.

It started several years ago when I, rather accidentally, picked out the perfect dress for Easter. The girls were searching frantically among the hordes of shoppers when I slipped around the corner to catch a moment of aloneness, in other words, to avoid the oncoming panic attack. I stood out of sight behind a clothes rack and the dress just caught my eye. I grabbed it, walked from behind my hiding place, and mimicking real shoppers said, "How about this one?"

She said "Yes" to the dress, and in that miraculous moment, I became the Papa with good taste.

Since then, we have shopped together for shoes (dress and casual), dresses, sweats, hoodies, and shorts. We even went shopping together for swimsuits. Actually, we were in Little Rock, and Charlotte called and said, "Why don't y'all look for a swimsuit while you're there?" Were you paying attention when I said she was almost 13?

First of all, I was the only male in the entire store (not Walmart), so every female in the universe was staring at me as I tried to find the bottoms to go with the top that my little granddaughter had picked out. Suddenly, she was no longer my little granddaughter. These were real swimsuits, if you know what I mean.

She carried two into the dressing room to try on, and I stood outside waiting on her with my eyes staring at my feet while every mom in the county glared at me. She came out of the dressing room and said in a mature voice that I had never heard, "Papa, these are both nice, they fit just right, and they are appropriate." I did not let her see the pair of overall shorts I had behind my back that I was going to suggest as an alternative. And then she said, "But I'm afraid they cost too much." I raised my head and made eye contact with every mom in the store and said, "If those are the ones you want, I will sell everything I own to make sure you have them." I didn't really say that, but my heart said it. What I really said was, "Get 'em and let's get out of here."

I didn't see her in the swimsuits until we got home. Everyone approved. She is a beautiful young lady, but I wanted to get in the truck, go back to the store, and get my little granddaughter, who apparently was still in that dressing room.

Chapter 15

Entertaining the Grands

Charlotte and I had the privilege of keeping our youngest granddaughters, who at the time were ages eight and six, for a whole week. It rained almost every day, so Walmart was my "go to" activity for fun and entertainment. I know how sad that sounds, but we live in a small town, and … I'm old.

Our first purchase was the board game, The Game of Life. Lessons we learned: paydays are important, children or no children is a roll of the dice, you can only get so many kids in one car, and the first one to retire wins. We played the game twice.

On our next fun trip, we cruised the toy aisles for 30 minutes before spotting the "newest, neatest, smells like a banana" toy called, Banana. "Smell it, Papa. What does it smell like?" I thought it smelled like $11 of cheap plastic, but I smiled and said enthusiastically, "Umm, banana." For those of you not familiar with this piece of creative genius, it is shaped like a banana and when opened, it contains a dozen tiny individual pieces wrapped in something like body armor. I used seven different attachments on the Swiss Army knife, but I finally had 24 small plastic pieces of something laying out on the cabinet. I could not identify one single item, but the girls knew what or who they were.

We made one more trip to Walmart and I promised them one more toy. We were there for close to an hour, but I loved every second. The eight-year-old made her selection quickly, but the six-year-old looked, touched, squeezed, admired, and pondered every toy on every aisle until finally making her choice. She chose exactly what her sister had chosen an hour earlier.

At the end of the week, we sent the girls home with plenty of leftover candy, cookies, cereal, and two large plastic bags full of tiny plastic somethings.

By the way, when we were checking out with the famous Banana toy, the checker said, "What are these things? Everyone seems to be wanting them." The rush is on, Walmart shoppers!

Chapter 16

Family Memories

I hope you're not too disappointed if this chapter is not about Walmart. I've written about almost everything I've ever observed at Walmart except the dress code, or lack of one, and honestly, I have no words. There are no words. Except that a friend told me that he overheard a conversation in Dollar General and the customer said they shop there "because you have to get dressed up to go to Walmart." My friend did not say what the customer was or was not wearing. Just keep that in mind … some people dress up to go to Walmart.

I was sitting in the waiting room of a doctor's office this week visiting with another old guy, when the conversation turned to our boyhood days. We both agreed that air conditioning and indoor toilets were great improvements, but there were some things that we both missed … like large family gatherings on Sundays after church.

Usually, these gatherings were at the home place of our grandparents, and usually they involved big porches, huge portions of home-cooked food, and large shade trees surrounded by homemade quilts. At some point during the afternoon, the kids would wait their turn to sit on a folded-up paper ice sack while Uncle Somebody cranked the wooden ice cream freezer. Fresh peach was always my favorite. There was always plenty of laughter and as the day drew to a close, children would be seen sitting closer and closer to their parents as if they were drawn there by an internal time clock. It was time to load up and begin the drive home.

I know that families still get together and still eat and laugh together, but today we seem to have more distractions. The days of my boyhood are gone, never to be seen again. There are new memories to be made with new generations of family members and, hopefully, they will look back with fondness and thankfulness for our new versions of family gatherings.

Personally, I'm convinced that the family gathering in heaven will be unlike anything any of us have experienced. We really don't know if there will be shade trees or ice cream, but we do know that the day will never end. I hope to see you there.

Chapter 17

Walmart Hallmark Movie?

I like to watch Hallmark movies! There, I've said it and I will not turn in my man card. Charlotte asked me why I liked them so much and I responded, "I am a romantic." She laughed out loud and was still laughing as she walked out of the room. I know they're not real to life because I've never seen one that involved anyone who moved back home to work at the local Walmart, nor have I ever seen any of the characters shopping at a Walmart. No one in a Hallmark movie ever says, "Hey, we must save our local bookstore, so let's have a festival with local people selling stuff, so run out to Walmart and get some cups and paper towels and bottled water to use for the 23 people who will attend."

The Hallmark script is always predictable. Loser Guy thinks he has Nice Girl locked into his idea of a self-serving relationship, but she goes back home to save Mom and Dad's failing bookstore because nobody buys books anymore. She runs into Nice Guy who has just moved back home and is in a relationship with Mean Girl. Loser Guy has no idea he is losing Nice Girl to Nice Guy, but Mean Girl sees what's happening and puts a plan in motion to create havoc. At some point, Nice Guy and Nice Girl will almost kiss, but will be interrupted, usually by Mean Girl.

Now, here is the most important part of the movie: there will always be some kind of false assumption, false accusation, or miscommunication that will jeopardize the chances of Nice Guy and Nice Girl actually kissing while snow is falling, even though there

51

has been no snow during the entire movie. However, true love always wins, and Nice Guy and Nice Girl do get to kiss as the snow falls and the movie ends. Mean Girl and Loser Guy seem to take their loss and humiliation in stride and hopefully, one day, they will be Nice Guy and Nice Girl, but I doubt it.

Since I am such a romantic (Charlotte laughs again), I would like to write a script for a Walmart Hallmark movie. There would be no "Almost Kiss," no snow, and no Loser Guy or Mean Girl, but there would be a false assumption and/or a misunderstanding. In the movie, entitled Love Goes Shopping, Nice Guy goes to Walmart to shop for Nice Girl. He has the list dictated to him by Nice Girl. Nice girl wants to make her special bean salad for the two of them to enjoy, so she asks for three different kinds of canned beans. Nice Guy finds two kinds of canned beans for the special salad, but has difficulty finding he third kind. He refers to his list one more time to make sure he is reading it correctly. Yes, "One can of Waxed Green beans" is written neatly on his list. Nice Guy looks and looks to no avail only to be later informed by disappointed Nice Girl that Waxed Green beans are actually yellow.

Now that is the kind of misunderstanding and lack of communication that keeps the snow from falling at the end of the movie. Oh well, life is not a Hallmark movie and Walmart is no place for a romantic ... and nobody gets kissed when they get home from Walmart.

Chapter 18

Shoppers on Vacation

Vacation time in our area means tons of visitors to our local Walmart. Because we are located just a few miles from a large lake and beautiful campgrounds, the aisles are usually filled with shoppers unfamiliar with the layout of our store and, obviously, unable to read the large overhead signs. It's comical to watch and listen as they yell, "Found it," to someone two aisles away.

I would say that most of these vacationers are probably not experienced travelers. I say this because they seem to have forgotten to pack clothing for any activities away from the boat or the swimming areas. Nothing gets you in the 4th of July spirit like watching flip-flop-clad strangers in sleep attire or swimwear (or some strange combination of the two) running through the store looking for charcoal and mustard. Seriously, people, pack some clothes!! You might actually see other people on your vacation—other people who are not interested in seeing so much of you.

You don't have to have a travel agent to experience a great vacation, but a little forethought might make your vacation more enjoyable for the rest of us. Think ahead. Ask yourself, "Will there be any time in the next five days when I will be in any public place where sleepwear/swimwear might be seen as questionable attire?" We're not snooty people here in Clark County, and we certainly don't have dress codes for Walmart shoppers, but most of us have enough common sense to ask ourselves before leaving the house, "If this is the last day of my life, do I want to stand before Holy God in this?" (Please no theological comments; I'm trying to make a point).

Our town motto is: "It's a great place to call home," and it is also a great place to visit. Please continue to vacation in our area, continue to enjoy the beautiful scenery, and please continue to shop at our local stores. We hope to see you again soon, just not quite as much of you. By the way, Walmart sells clothes appropriate for all occasions.

Note: For those vacationers who may be new to our area—they're called red bugs or "chiggers" and they are especially angry this time of year. If you scratch really hard, they will go away.

Chapter 19

The Procedure

I have not been to Walmart in eight days. That is a new record for my post-retirement days, since becoming the primary grocery shopper person in our family. I have also not been out of the house since July 3rd, when I had a "procedure" done on my left knee. The outpatient "procedure" is called a knee arthroscopy. It was explained to me like this: "We will place two-to-four tiny holes on the outside of your knee to clean out the torn and frayed meniscus. We will send you home on crutches for two-three days with instructions for at-home therapy." I am not trying to frighten or discourage anyone who might benefit from this procedure, nor am I questioning anyone who has breezed through the procedure with few or no issues. I'm just telling you what I have experienced so far.

First, this is surgery! Look it up: pro-ce-dure: "a surgical operation." I knew this was going to be more than just a "procedure" the moment the nurse said, "Take off everything but your underwear." After the IV was properly inserted, the nurse gave me my first injection. "What was that injection for?" I asked. "It was to wipe out your short-term memory," she replied nonchalantly. "What was that injection for?" I asked. I thought that was funny, but apparently attempts at humor are not allowed when you're being prepared for a "procedure."

The next indication that this was more than a "procedure" was when the nurse placed me on an ironing board. Beds that small are not used for "procedures." Then there was the mask placed over my mouth with the instructions, "This is just oxygen. Take four deep breaths and then breathe normally." That was not "just oxygen!!" I've had oxygen and it enabled me to catch my breath and get back in the game, not take me out and leave me totally defenseless, lying on an ironing board in my underwear. Since we live about an hour from where the "procedure" was performed, the ride home in the back seat of my truck was memorable. I had asked the anesthesiologist to knock me out until Sunday morning church time, but once again, attempts at humor are not appropriate during a "procedure."

Now I know there are pros and cons about being six-feet five-inches tall, but trying to maneuver back and forth through the house with two crutches the size of cell towers under your armpits takes some strength and coordination … which I no longer have. Our dog is scared to death of the cell towers and his lengthy naps in our bathroom have been constantly interrupted. "Drink lots of water," they told me. Sure, so you will have to hobble back and forth every 45 minutes and wear out your other knee. By the way, I still cannot bend my knee to sit. I'm not meaning to cross the line here, but how do women deal with this?

My five-day "post-procedure" checkup went well and I'm progressing right on schedule. I'm not experiencing much pain, except for my armpits. As I hobbled out of the exam room after the checkup, the waiting room was filled with anxious patients waiting to find out their medical futures. All eyes were focused on my knee, which looked a lot like "Wilson" at the end of the movie, *Cast Away*. One lady recognized me and asked if I had something done to my knee.

"Yeah," I replied, "I had a procedure."

Hopefully, I will be back in the aisles of Walmart soon and the dog can get back into his routine.

Chapter 20

Missing the People

It has now been over two weeks since I have visited our local Walmart. The knee "procedure" has kept me down, and partially out. This would have been the perfect time for us to become acquainted with the "Free Grocery Pickup" offered by our local store, but we chose instead to allow our son and grandson to "pick up some things" for us. Their service also was free.

At the risk of sounding like I'm too heavily medicated, I must confess that I miss my trips to Walmart. I know the day will probably come when the Free Grocery Pickup option will be a necessity and not a choice. But for as long as I physically can, I am going to drive the 1.3 miles, park in the same aisle when possible, cringe when I see grown adults walk through a door that clearly says 'Exit," follow the same shopping patterns ... always beginning with paper goods and laundry detergent before heading to the back of the store for milk and eggs, and cautiously search and hunt every aisle while trying to accomplish my goal of getting the right kind and right size of everything on my list, and making it home with everything we will need, without having to return to the store for at least 48 hours. That may sound silly and petty to some, but I have accepted the self-imposed challenge of completing at least one perfect shopping experience before I go to heaven. If I were a mom or dad that had to shop with small children, "Free Grocery Pickup" would seem like the greatest thing since the installation of lights at Wrigley

Field. I would probably be relieved and rejoicing that I did not have to shop and supervise at the same time.

In full disclosure, I confess to you that I am an introvert. "Free Grocery Pickup" is designed for a guy like me, and it is a huge temptation, but I have noticed in the last fifteen days that the one thing I miss about my Walmart trips is the people, and my head is clear as I write this. Every time I'm in our local store, I'm reminded of how much I need others and how much others need me. In other words, God made us to be relational, and we really do need each other. I've had some wonderful divine appointments in the aisles of Walmart when a brief encounter has led to a spiritual conversation or just a positive word about the goodness of God. Prayer requests are sometimes shared openly in those aisles, and I can't remember leaving the store many times without being prompted to pray for someone I've seen or for something I've heard.

I spent years "prayer walking" the streets of cities and villages all over the world … praying on site, with insight. I was honored to pray for people as we passed each other on a crowded street or in a busy market, people I did not know and likely will never know. It is highly possible that I was the first person who had ever prayed specifically for them. Think about that!

In recent years, I am receiving the same promptings as I make my way through the Walmart aisles. I pray that they might know how much God loves them. I pray for their peace, for their deliverance, for their health, and … I know, this is beginning to sound like a sermon.

I think, as soon as I can recover from this "procedure," that I will continue to make my trips to Walmart, and continue my goal of achieving one perfect shopping trip before I "check out." It wouldn't be perfect without praying on site with insight. Blessings!

Chapter 21

Still Recovering

Three weeks after the knee "procedure" and I am still in recovery mode. No Walmart visits. However, I have made three PT visits. Physical Therapy is a painful necessity and a reminder that if you ever, ever, had a cuss word pass through your mind for even a fleeting second, that word may still be buried and hidden away, and could very well burst forth in a not-so-silent groan that compromises the "God is good all the time" conversation you just had with the nice lady on the recumbent exercise equipment. Charlotte refers to this as "head cussing," but my slip was more "heard" than "head." I publicly apologize to all the churches I have pastored, and to the nice lady who did not judge me, although I'm pretty sure I will be an addition to someone's prayer list, hopefully, an "unspoken request."

Honestly, the word escaped before I was even conscious that it was being formed. It was never "on the tip of my tongue." Instead, it was unearthed and sprang out of my mouth like one of those jack in the boxes that frightens children, and then, just dangles there with a "gotcha" smirk that makes you want to stuff it back down and close the lid on it again. Sometimes those kinds of words and thoughts will spring up and pop out, and smirk at us. I'd like to blame this one on the physical therapy, but I know who cranked it out.

I can think of one other embarrassing occasion when words (not cuss words) sprang up out of nowhere. It was not a Walmart experience, but a Pet Store experience. I had been sent on a solo mission to find a replacement toy for our beloved Corgi, Cubbie. Solo shopping is not my spiritual gift, and it seldom ends well. You would think that even Cubbie, unleashed in a pet store, could find one specific item, but after thirty minutes of hunting, I reverted to every man's greatest fear, and asked for help. The nice, bearded, pierced, twenty-something young man listened patiently as I tried to describe a dog toy. Finally, he said, "Do you have a picture?" I've owned a smart phone for a decade and still cannot remember that I carry our photo album in my pocket. After looking at several pictures of Cubbie and his favorite toy, he was kind enough to leave his behind-the-counter workstation and go all the way to the stock room to see if they had that toy. He returned shaking his head and was sincerely disappointed when he reported that, "We must be out of those."

What happened next is hard to explain. I really appreciated his interest and willingness to help me and genuinely wanted to express my appreciation for his efforts. Before my mind was synchronized with my mouth, I looked him in the eye and from the bottom of my heart said, "Good dog." It just popped out and dangled there, smirking. The nice young man tilted his head and just looked at me like … well, like Cubbie looks when I am speaking human words to him and all he really wants is for me to find his lost toy. I turned and walked away and have never returned to any pet store.

Today, I will return to Physical Therapy and to the necessary pain involved with complete recovery, but I will attempt to keep a lid on my improper and embarrassing outbursts.

Chapter 22

Mom and Pork Chops

Fifty-three years ago, a man walked on the moon. Fifty-three years ago, I got married. Fifty-three years ago, I was privileged to play on a Conference Championship football team at Henderson State University. Fifty-three years ago, my mother bought groceries at the B&B Grocery in Hope, Arkansas. The store had two checkout counters, three short aisles of groceries, and a nice meat counter at the back of the store. She bought groceries there every Friday afternoon because that was payday. My mom departed this life in 1984, thirty-eight years ago, and to my knowledge she never shopped in a Walmart.

If I could talk to her today, I would tell her that Neil Armstrong really did walk on the moon (she never believed it was real), that she was so right about Charlotte (she is who I needed), that I appreciate, more than ever, the fact that she never missed a sporting event in which I played, and that this new thing called "Walmart grocery pickup" is "one giant leap for mankind." Especially, if you are recovering from knee surgery and can't take many steps.

I'm not sure my mom would have allowed anyone else to pick out her pork chops, but I think she would be impressed with the idea of pulling up to a reserved parking spot and watching as a friendly employee places your completed grocery list into your car.

Explaining this process to Mom would be like the Apostle John writing the book of Revelation and trying to describe futuristic images with contemporary vocabulary. "Well, Mom, we had to download the App onto our Smart Phones and then, it's just a matter of scrolling through each department and clicking onto a picture of each item. You put each item into your cart and then you pay with your card number. They send you a text to let you know when to pick up your groceries and then they track your car to let them know when you arrive." How would I explain that experience to my mother, thirty-eight years ago?

"I, Stan, saw a man with a miniature TV in one hand (about the size of Dad's billfold; Dad never owned a wallet), viewing and typing at the same time. He was picking out groceries, like picking out Christmas presents from the Sears catalog, except the people at Sears knew which items he was selecting. When his wish list was complete, he typed in his bank information and trusted them to take just that amount from his account. People in the store, obviously watching the same channel, knew what he wanted from the pictures he had checked, and they retrieved each item from the shelves, bagged them up and saved it for him. Here's the weird part … they knew where his miniature TV was at all times, like they were watching him through the screen. When he drove up, he did not have to get out and come in, they knew he was there, and they brought his groceries to his car."

After hearing this prophetic description, my mom would say, "Sure. And you believe that a man walked on the moon." She would also say, "I'm not trusting anyone at Sears to pick out my pork chops."

Chapter 23

Agony of Defeat

I found a parking place right next to the 12 prime spots that have been reserved for Walmart grocery pickup. Those 12 spots are center aisle, closest to the building; the parking places that a lot of us start looking for the second we pull into the parking lot. The kind of parking places that my wife always prays for and usually finds.

I decided that my knee was still not ready for the challenges of Walmart, especially since school supplies were the primary reason for this midafternoon trip. So, I sat in the truck while Charlotte and our then-seventh grade granddaughter and all others entered the store through the exit doors, looking back over their shoulders and laughing. I get no respect.

What I witnessed for the next thirty minutes was very similar to the old *Wide World of Sports* intro ..." the thrill of victory and the agony of defeat." Car after car entered the parking lot, caught a glimpse of all the vacant spots right down front, and sped toward the gift from heaven, only to be disappointed by the bright, orange, *Reserved for Pickup* signs.

Each driver was laser focused, hands at ten and two, speeding toward the grand prize, and then, the *Reserved* signs would appear, and the perfect parking place mirage would disappear, and their shoulders would slump, and even their cars seemed to stall in disappointment.

What a cruel joke to play on loyal customers, I thought. It kind of reminded me of boarding an airplane and having to walk through First Class on your way back to the seat closest to the restroom door. A few folks, after surviving the disappointment of the phantom parking spot, found available parking places some distance away, and walked grudgingly past the First Class Reserved Section. One gentleman stopped in the middle of one of the choice spots, looked back across the parking lot at where he had parked his car, and just shook his head. I have no idea what he was thinking, but I know what I was thinking. "Why? Why choose those prime parking places for pickup?"

Oh, well, there are more important concerns in the world, like how long does it take to buy school supplies? And why am I enjoying watching all these people experiencing the agony of defeat? And who wrote Hebrews? And why 12 spots? And who came up with the infield fly rule? And why does my mind work like this, or not?

Life is not fair, and once you know that life is not fair, it's not as hard to walk across a hot parking lot, pick up your own groceries, check yourself out, bag your own groceries, walk back across the lot, load the groceries into your car, and realize, hey, at least I'm not going into the seventh grade. Life is good.

Chapter 24

The Truth of Absence

It has been over a month since the last Walmart Words post. Clark County rumors explaining my silence include my having received a letter of intimidation and warning from Walmart Headquarters, and having received an offer for a publishing contract. Neither rumor is true, but it kind of points out how slow life can be in small towns while we wait for football season.

The truth is that I have not been too motivated to write because of life. Life can, at times, interrupt my ability to see humor. The senseless, despicable shooting at the El Paso Walmart in early August probably altered the thought processes of many of us as we entered the Walmart doors over the next weeks. Yet, another reminder that life on earth is fragile.

One week later, I sat at the hospital bedside of my first cousin and listened to his confidence in the providence of God and the promises of Holy Scripture. Just a few hours later, he departed this life peacefully as his children stood by his side. He asked me to "speak at his funeral," which, for a minister, is one of the greatest honors of our calling. This was another reminder that life on earth is short.

Today, I was back at our local Walmart searching for my Honey Nut Cheerios and looking for the next story. It was my first real shopping trip since my infamous knee procedure, and it felt good to be back in the narrow, crowded aisles of Walmart.

All the players were there today. The guy with his cart parked in the middle of the aisle as he peered through trifocals in an attempt to read the small print on a hot sauce label ... he was there. We were all blocked and backed up like a school pickup line as he took forever to make his selection The designated "Walmart pickup" shoppers were there. So were new employees, who pile six rows of blue plastic containers on a cart and attempt to maneuver it through the store without the ability to see over, around, or through the filled containers. Since they can't see you anyway, they have no reservation or remorse about slamming into you or parking those oversized carts, leaving them abandoned while searching for items on the next aisle over. I wanted to hijack one of those abandoned monstrosities and hide it in the back storage area, but I knew I would blow out my other knee trying to push it.

The older gentleman, the one who uses his iPhone to make his shopping list and then accidentally deletes everything on the list just as he makes it to the second aisle, was also there, but had to leave early. Another reminder that life is funny.

Note: In case you missed it ... I'm that guy.

Chapter 25

Wait for the Beep

For those of you who did not pick up on the poorly written last paragraph of my last entry, I was the older gentleman who "accidentally deleted everything on his list." For that reason, I was back in the aisles on a very busy Friday afternoon to pick up the deleted items. It was chaos!

Walmart shoppers filling up their blue bins for folks in the designated pickup parking spots were scrambling and darting all over the store with those oversized carts. Obviously, Friday afternoon is the prime time for pickup shopping; there were at least a dozen employees busily trying to fill orders and meet the deadline. I have made a practice of asking these designated shoppers if they are new employees and so far, all of them have said that they were recently hired for this specific job assignment. That's good news. The bad news is that it appears that some of them have never shopped at Walmart. Today, one of the young shoppers was so frustrated that she asked me for help … me! "Sir, do you know where the Cuties are?" she asked. I wanted to say that fifty years ago, I always knew where they were, but I knew that my attempt at humor would not be understood or appreciated. "I think you'll find them next to the oranges," I told her, but I was thinking how ironic that anyone would ask me how to find anything in Walmart.

I was already distracted and about to panic because the checkout lines were stacked up six deep, forcing me to attempt the self-checkout with mangoes and avocados. In times past, my attempts to self-check fruit have ended in disaster. I was so nervous that I dropped a mango onto the floor trying to open one of those sorry, cheap, plastic bags. I hate those bags!

Arriving at the self-checkout, I was less than self-confident, but I tried to give the appearance that I knew what I was doing, especially since I was surrounded by college students. I scanned the easy stuff first, hoping the entire store would be vacated when I came to the fruit. Suddenly, my checkout thingy was flashing red and immediately, a nice young employee rushed to my side. "What did you just scan?" she asked. "Uh, uh, uh, Delsym cough syrup," I said. She punched in some numbers, and swiped her store ID card. "The machine says you're too young to purchase cough syrup," she said with a smile. The college students found that amusing. I just wanted them to leave before I got to the fruit. The nice young employee offered to scan the remaining items in my cart, and I casually said, "Sure, that would be nice." Inside, I was screaming out, "Thank you, God! Thank you! Thank you!"

The only remaining steps were to insert my debit card and remember where I had parked my truck. I inserted the card, followed the promptings, and waited for the little beep sound to "Remove the card." When I heard the beep, I pulled out the card and the checkout thingy was once again flashing. As it turned out, the beeping sound I heard was not the signal to remove my card … it was the lady behind me in her electric shopping cart. The college kids left with a great story and I left with a beeping sound in my ear that won't go away.

Chapter 26

The Things You Hear in Line

I have mentioned several times the uniqueness of our local Walmart with the addition of 3,000-plus university students in our small community. We love having them in our community, in our churches, and in Walmart's self-checkout lines. They always use self-checkout, the positive side of that being that it makes the old school checkout lines a little less congested for the rest of us. However, I do think these young students could benefit from standing in line with humanity and participating in everyday Walmart conversations. There are no college majors that could possibly impart information as valuable as standing in a checkout line and listening-in on a Walmart conversation.

I cannot risk divulging some of the wisdom I have heard while waiting to check out because I know these people and they know where I live. I must maintain their confidence, or the conversations could cease. Local people are already skeptical of being seen by me in Walmart. The joy of Walmart shopping (strange phrase) is seeing real people being human. The good, the bad, and the not so attractive are all part of our world and we all have in common the fact that we were created by God, and we were created for relationships, and that is why college students need to get out of the self-checkout lines of the world and get an education.

One day they will need to know how a kind smile and a simple "how are you doing" can make a person's day. The day may also come when they need to know how to grow tomatoes and potatoes and I have heard many different successful strategies while waiting in checkout lines. I know that you can "YouTube" instructions for almost anything, but I prefer listening to someone explain how to smoke a pork tenderloin while I'm looking them in the eye. It seems to me that the meat tastes better with the personal touch.

The whole idea of "self" anything bothers me. Oh, I get it, the need to have some space and some alone time, but that is different from determined isolation from the rest of humanity, or at least the part of humanity that is not just like me. The fact that I could put in my earbuds, shop while listening to my playlist, and check myself out without ever making eye contact or speaking to the dozens of human beings within arms' reach does not seem like progress to me ... and I am not just talking about college students. So, use the self-serving opportunities cautiously and always seize the opportunities to smile and ask me how I'm doing.

You may just make my day.

Let no unwholesome word proceed from your mouth, but only such a word as is good for edification according to the need of the moment, so that it will give grace to those who hear. (Ephesians 4:29 NASB)

Chapter 27

Christmas Treasure Shopping

Well, it's Christmastime at Walmart! I know, it has been since early October in most stores, but now the shelves are full of "bargain" decorations and the aisles are full of bargain hunters.

My wife can purchase $6 worth of "bargain" decorations and turn them into a wreath that will be the envy of the neighborhood. So, she promised our granddaughter one of her award-winning wreaths for her front door and here I am in "Decorations Unlimited" where the estrogen levels are reaching record highs.

I have chosen to park the cart on one aisle and allow Charlotte to browse the crowded aisles alone, partly because I can't keep up with her when she's on a mission, and partly because of the estrogen overload in that space. Charlotte has several different shopping speeds and I'm able to shift gears and stay close most of the time, but not when she is in "on-a-mission" speed.

Presently, I am the only male on this aisle and if I have heard, "Get it now or it won't be here later" once, I have heard it a dozen times. I want to shout at the top of my voice, "If it's up to me this stuff will still be here long after Santa Claus is resting comfortably back home in January!" But I love to be alive, so I just stand here and force a smile.

Charlotte has found a few items that will magically become a family treasure and she gently places them in our cart which already contains—and I am not making this up—weed killer, weed eater line, bug fogger, batteries, pita bread, a can of 2-cycle fuel for small engines, bar soap, a broom, and a small ham. We had not yet added the cilantro, asparagus, and my Honey Nut Cheerios. Ho! Ho! Ho! Merry Christmas.

Chapter 28

Quail Hunting Memories

It was just another quick run to Walmart to pick up essentials like bread, milk, cereal, and maraschino cherries (needed for a special recipe). It was a busy Friday afternoon and the store was crowded with deer hunters and an unusual number of university students. In addition to the high volume of shoppers, Walmart employees were stocking shelves on every aisle. Rudeness was everywhere. The whole world was in a hurry. I'm sure you can identify when I say that this was not a pleasant shopping experience.

I had weaved my way through the madness and was headed toward the finish line when I spotted a guy who looked as miserable as I was at that moment. He was dressed in camo, so I said what anyone would say in our Walmart this time of year: "Did you get the big one yet?" For those of you who live on the left or right coast, I was asking him if he had killed (harvested) a big buck deer.

His response stopped me in my tracks and filled me with such emotion that I wanted to grab him and hug him right in front of the Fuji apples. In one brief statement, this stranger took me back 50-plus years to memories that warmed my heart and could have very easily resulted in an embarrassing outpouring of tears.

They say that with age emotions are easily triggered, but I don't know anything about that … I'm only 73. He said to me in a South Arkansas accent that is music to my ears, "I don't deer hunt anymore; I'm a quail hunter." A quail hunter!!! We pulled our shopping carts over by the sweet potatoes and he told me all about his quail hunting trips to Kansas, both of us expressing our sadness that quail hunting in Arkansas is a thing of the past. We talked about the sound of a covey rise, how quickly they get up and how fast they fly, the excitement of watching the dogs working together, and the taste of fried quail. We both agreed there is nothing better.

I thought back to my boyhood, of my hunting buddies, of those wonderful dogs, of quail for breakfast on Christmas morning, of my mother's biscuits and gravy. I asked if he had a picture of his dogs. He did and they looked just like I hoped they would. We parted ways without ever introducing ourselves, but we were both smiling, and what had been a not-so-enjoyable trip to Walmart had become an experience that brought back tucked-away memories that still make me smile. I'm thankful for those memories, and I know what I want for Christmas.

Chapter 29
Remembering That Smile

Today, I was honored to participate in the memorial service of a sweet mom, teacher, wife, and committed follower of Christ. She, in her 50 years of life, had earned the admiration and respect of our community. To say that she was well-loved would be an obvious understatement. Many stories and memories were shared today, and I certainly have her sweet smile etched in my mind along with the memory of one of the most pleasant people I have ever known.

I thought about her late this afternoon as I pulled into the Walmart parking lot. I can still see her in my mind as she stood by a cart full of groceries, waved to me, and said, "Can you wait until I put my groceries in the car so I can follow you around Walmart?" She loved reading these stories. She loved me. If you knew her, she loved you. She loved our dog. If you have a dog, she loved your dog. Her departure from this life came suddenly and unexpectedly, but her impact will be long lasting.

So, as I entered the very busy, super-crowded Walmart, I wanted to be upset with the two employees who had parked themselves right in front of the cans of pumpkin to carry on their conversation, but I could not. I could not lose my patience with those shoppers who seem to find it impossible to push a cart in a straight line, or those who do not yield, or stop at the end of the aisle to display courtesy.

I could not be anything but pleasant today, and that is not my usual Walmart attitude. I kept thinking about Christy's desire to "follow me around Walmart," and in my mind I could see her pleasant smile. It was such a nice smile. It amazes me that a genuine, happy smile can have such impact. I won't see her anymore at Walmart, at least not physically, but I remember where she was parked that day when she was unloading her cart and I will always think of her at that spot, and maybe, just maybe, I can be more pleasant as I wander through the aisles of Walmart.

I will see her again in heaven. I'm sure of that, and that makes me smile. Have a pleasant Thanksgiving.

Chapter 30

Sports Illustrated and THE Game

News that the national magazine, *Sports Illustrated*, was in town covering the Battle of the Ravine created a lot of excitement in our community. The in-depth, well-written article is in the latest issue of the magazine, and it accurately highlights the rivalry between Henderson State University and Ouachita Baptist University. If you live or have ever lived in Arkansas, you have heard of the oldest rivalry in Division II football. Find a copy of *Sports Illustrated* and read the article.

But you will not find it at our local Walmart. The magazines were moved to the very back of the store in a recent remodel and apparently all but hunting and women's magazines were lost in the move. It's a shame because they could have sold a thousand copies of *Sports Illustrated* when the news broke that the article was included in the current issue.

Our son, Kyle, and I are mentioned in the article because of our "blended family" status in the HSU vs. OBU rivalry, and yes, we do want a copy or two of the magazine. Our names are in *Sports Illustrated*! Although, it was pointed out to me by an OBU professor that I'm mentioned because of pastoring athletes and not so much because of having been an athlete. I'm okay with that; my name is in *Sports Illustrated*!

The young man who wrote the article was from Brooklyn and that ain't in Arkansas. I would have loved to have taken him to Walmart, but being an experienced writer, he didn't run out of anything he needed from Walmart during his visit. Do they even have Walmart in Brooklyn? Even if they do, I think he would still have been impressed with our version. I'll bet he's never seen big screen TV's and deer corn in the same display.

The week he was in town was the same week we had collards and turnip greens in the same huge bin in the vegetable area. If that's not impressive enough, there were neatly packaged hog jowls on top of the display. I would have loved to have walked him down the complete aisle of women's camo, but he never got to experience our Walmart.

He did, however, go to church with us on Sunday and he seemed to find it strange that two rivals could come together in harmony for worship. He sat with Kyle and me and noted that some worshippers seemed happier than others, but I have no comment about that. After all, football is not that important anyway … that's what we say in a losing year.

We took him to lunch (*Sports Illustrated* bought my lunch) and he had very nice things to say about our community. I think he would have also been impressed with our Walmart, but not with the magazine rack at the very back of the store, which does not contain one single issue of the *Sports Illustrated* with my name in it.

Chapter 31

Shopping at Atwoods

My search for a lawnmower battery took me from Walmart, which did not have what I needed, to Atwoods. If you've never been to an Atwoods, find the one nearest to you and take the family. I would describe this store as the farm family's general store with free popcorn. We shop often at Atwoods, but when I'm walking around in the store, I kind of feel like a "wannabe."

Should we ever experience a national Zombie Apocalypse, I will make a mad dash to Atwoods! I don't even know what most of the stuff is in the store, but it just looks like something needed for survival. Everything needed to garden, to farm, to hunt, to raise animals, to feed animals, and everything needed to wear to do all of the above … it's all there.

I could walk around this store for hours trying to look like I belong, but in my mind, I am saying, "What's that?" "What's that?" "What's that?" Everything in the store just looks so useful, but I don't know why.

I saw a family shopping and I watched them as they completed their shopping list. They knew what they needed, where to find it in the store, and seemed to know what it was all for. They had a baby boy about six-months old and the mama was talking to him in baby talk:

"Mama's boy is gonna be a bull rider, yeah, Mama's boy is gonna be a bull rider." The kid proceeded to spit up on Mama's cowgirl shirt. I would have done the same thing. I still have nightmares about being thrown from the back of a Shetland pony when I was 12. The only way you could get me on the back of a bull is if that was the only way to get to Atwoods during a Zombie Apocalypse.

I wish I knew more about farming and fixing stuff, but honestly, should that apocalypse occur, and should I find a way to make it to Atwoods, my only hope of survival would be to wrap myself in horse blankets and hide in one of those chicken coop thingies.

I put my lawnmower battery in the cart and walked around pretending for a while. At checkout, I took my battery out of the cart and placed it on the counter. The lady in line behind me seemed amused as she stood watching me. She was toting two 20-pound bags of dog food on her shoulders.

While browsing through the store, I did see some things that would make good Christmas presents ... for somebody.

Chapter 32

Christmas Memories

Christmas is coming and thoughts of Christmases past abound.

Even though there were no Walmart stores when I grew up just outside of Hope, the season was always full of gifts … and now wonderful visions of days gone by. It seems to me that Christmas memories are the longest-lasting memories.

The first Christmas present I remember was a child's wooden toolbox (those who know me best can go ahead and laugh). I was about three or four years old. My parents had a small dairy farm, which meant they were up at 4:30 a.m. every day to milk cows before they went to work. They felt comfortable letting me sleep until they finished their morning chores, but on that Christmas morning, I awoke early, looking for what Santa Claus had left for me under the tree. When I saw that toolbox, I just couldn't wait for my parents to see it. So, I carefully made my way down the steep, wooden, icy steps and walked barefooted the 30 yards to the dairy barn behind our house. To my surprise, my parents were not as excited about my present and neither were they excited to see me standing there barefooted on a cold winter morning. I can still hear my dad saying, "Bett (short for Betty), get that baby and get him back in the house!"

I also remember the day my world was rocked when my cousin showed me a shiny, new bicycle hidden in the back of the hay barn. I was seven years old; he was 12, and I've never forgiven him. I was not emotionally ready to learn about Santa Claus. I didn't let my cousin see me, but later, I cried.

As I grew older, we rarely made it to Christmas morning without opening every present under the tree. It would start about a week before Christmas, as we sat at the supper table … I would say, "After supper, how about we open one apiece." My mother would object, but my dad would chime in and eventually we would all rush into the living room and dig out one present each. We never saved anything for Christmas morning and the real fun was convincing Mother every year to "give in," which became easier and easier. Charlotte says I must remind everyone that I am an only child, but I don't understand what that's got to do with it.

My Aunt Belle was notorious for giving the same Christmas gift year after year. She loved to crochet, so every year she would supply our family with crocheted house slippers, and slippery they were. She would use thick, heavy, rug yarn so they would last until next Christmas. Not only were they slippery, but the thick yarn also hurt the bottoms of your feet.

At my parents' house one Christmas, our three children were sliding and falling all over the house and when they took off Aunt Belle's slippers, they literally had yarn imprints on the bottoms of their feet. Back in my parents' bedroom, out of Aunt Belle's hearing, I asked my dad, "What are we going to do with these things?" He grinned, opened the closet door, pointed to years of crocheted slippers piled up in the back of the closet, and said, "Pitch 'em in here with these." I've never laughed as hard in my entire life.

Growing up, I could always count on a stocking filled with apples, oranges, and an assortment of nuts. I always knew that my presents would include six pairs of underwear and six T-shirts. Mother loved to outline the picture window in front of the house with large blue lights. The foil-covered front door depicting a large Santa Claus was always part of our Christmas decorations and we always had a real cedar Christmas tree. Mother's famous peppermint cake and what she called "date-nut roll" were annual treats. I can still feel the warmth of the kitchen, smell parched peanuts in the oven, and hear Mother shaking them in the metal pan to keep them from burning. Cracking and picking out pecans was a family project in the evenings as Dad and I drooled just thinking about the Karo-nut pie that would soon come out of the oven.

Like I said, Christmas memories are the longest-lasting memories. As I think back on boyhood Christmases, I don't think about the gifts as much as I think about a warm house, a warm kitchen, and, thanks to Aunt Belle, warm feet. I hope our children and grandchildren will have wonderful memories that will warm their hearts when they are in their 70s.

Merry Christmas.

Chapter 33

Dangerous End-Caps!

Happy New Year! Personally, I am still recovering from the shopping madness of the holidays. At our house, holidays translate into lots of cooking and lots of Walmart trips—not your normal trips, but trips for very specific items … things like bay leaves, white Karo, dark chocolate, dark brown sugar, golden raisins, apple cider vinegar, unpeeled and uncooked shrimp, etc. To make things even more complicated, there are requests for specific sizes and amounts of all kinds of things for all kinds of specific recipes. I am still such an amateur.

Of course, to complicate matters even more, our entire state shares the same recipes requiring the exact same ingredients. So, Walmart only puts on the shelves enough of those specific items to meet the specific needs of one or two large families. The rest of us are doomed to stagger up and down every aisle looking for what they call "end-caps."

For example, I don't understand why the cereals needed for the traditional Chex-mix cannot be placed on the shelf with the rest of the cereals. Why must it be placed in an end-cap six aisles away, next to the international foods? And, by the way, end-caps are extremely dangerous. Trying to get an item from an end-cap is kind of like the old video game, Frogger, and you're the frog.

While I'm mentioning complications with holiday shopping, those platform ladders used by Walmart employees are really a problem. I've seen smaller scaffolding at building sites. I'm convinced that they place them in front of the most popular items on an aisle, leave them there unattended, and go to the in-store camera monitors just to watch the traffic jams.

Of course, there is always the issue of an over-crowded store full of shoppers who are totally unaware that other people live on this planet. I am always aware of what's going on around me. Maybe it comes from years of international travel or being re-sponsible for teams of volunteers in high-risk areas. Maybe it is a result of being a defensive back in football and always looking for the large lineman, who wanted to knock me out. Or maybe, just maybe, I understand that my cart is not the only cart in the universe and that we all have the same recipes and must share the bay leaves.

I am thinking about designing two new T-shirts for the com-ing new year:

You Ain't The Only Cart On The Aisle!

I Survived Walmart End-Caps!

Chapter 34

Half-off Survival

It's amazing to me how different the atmosphere can be in our local Walmart, depending on the day and time of your visit. For example, I was in Walmart with my wife the day after Christmas. That's right, the day after Christmas! For those of you who have never had that experience, allow me to describe the scene in as few words as possible.

All Christmas decorations were 50 percent off. I stood in huddled horror next to my cart. I did not dare risk taking the cart into the jammed-packed aisles. I stood a good distance away, out of danger, and shielded from the rush and crush of humanity by my trusty cart. I watched fearfully as my wife said to me, "You stay here; I'm going in." When she disappeared into the crowded aisle, I immediately lost sight of her and wished I had said something different to her other than, "You're nuttier than squirrel poop if you go in there."

I stood there on my tiptoes trying to catch just a glimpse of her, but it was impossible to accurately identify anyone; they were moving too fast. From my safe zone, I had clear sight of three aisles and guesstimated there to be about forty individuals darting back and forth from aisle to aisle. A friend walked by and asked, "Are you here with Charlotte?" They seemed to share my concern when I motioned with a nod and replied, "She's in there." Charlotte did eventually reappear with arms full of bargains and with her sweet smile still in place. I was just thankful to see her alive with no injuries.

In contrast, I was in the same store, at about the same time, on New Year's Day. There were very few shoppers, but there were six checkout lanes open for business. The checkers were standing, smiling, and waiting for customers. I had a wonderful, leisurely conversation with the nice checker lady in Lane 4. As it turns out, she had received Christ as her Savior during 2019 and she asked me to pray for her husband, who had been diagnosed with cancer. She teared up when I mentioned that we were one year closer to Jesus' coming and closer to heaven than we've ever been.

On my way out, I was greeted by another employee who asked about our Christmas, our family, and politely inquired about Charlotte's back pain (I am a regular at our local store). It was a wonderful trip to Walmart. Now, if I just didn't have to go back until next New Year's Day. That seems to be the ideal day to shop at Walmart.

I'm certain my next shopping day will be much more hectic. Meanwhile, we're closer to heaven than we've ever been. And the nice lady in check-out lane 4 and I are both prepared.

Chapter 35

An "Invisible" Ride

The conversation did not take place in Walmart, but it could have because I've heard similar discussions in the aisles there. But, on this day I was in an elevator when two ladies entered and continued their conversation as if they had stayed in the spot where they started talking. I won't venture a guess where that may have been or how long they had been talking. Even though I was standing there—and I am not hard to see at 6'5"—the conversation continued as if the two of them were alone on the planet.

I no longer attempt to guess ages, but it's safe to say that I was the youngest person on the elevator. The conversation was about the complications of irritable bowel syndrome, which it seems both ladies had experienced. They were standing facing each other just in front of me, but I appeared to be invisible as the conversation moved from symptoms to treatment. Never has an elevator seemed so small!

The elevator reached their floor, the doors opened, and just before exiting one of the ladies said, "Since Charles passed away four years ago, my IBS has cleared up and gone away." Then, for the first time my presence was acknowledged and as they exited; they turned to me and one of them said with a smile, "No offense intended, but you men cause a lot of stress."

"Yes, ma'am," I said, "I've been paying attention for four floors." The doors closed and I thought to myself, "I bet Charles is one happy fellow."

It is amazing how many lessons I learned in such a short ride:

- I now know more about IBS than I ever wanted to know.

- There is no way off of a moving elevator.

- I have serious questions about the circumstances of Charles' passing.

- Discussion of medical conditions and symptoms in the presence of others should be a felony.

- There should be a volume control button for elevator music, including a "very loud" option.

- Walking the aisles of Walmart is much safer than riding in elevators.

- Never create a stress-filled life for your wife. Uh … oh, no!

Chapter 36

Neighborhood Market

I visited a big city a couple of weeks ago and discovered something called a Walmart Neighborhood Market. As I approached the store, I was very impressed that the exit doors would not, I repeat, would not open from the outside. As I entered, a quick head-turn to my left revealed that you must, I repeat, must exit through the exit door. Great!

I also noticed that the color scheme was different—a brighter green that seemed to guarantee fresher fruit, fresher vegetables, and the most current products. The carts were newer. The aisles were wider. The store was smaller ... I'm told about one-fifth the size of a Walmart Supercenter. The store was not as crowded as our local Walmart and I must admit that shopping was relatively stress-free.

After about ten minutes, I began to think, "This ain't no Walmart!" (That's the way I think, but, thanks to my sixth-grade teacher, not the way I speak.) These people didn't even know each other. There were no "block-the-aisle conversations." Nobody was sharing prayer requests or asking about someone's knee replacement. There were no college students shopping in groups of six trying to figure out how many hot dogs to grill for a party. Honestly, it was kind of boring. I greeted another shopper with a head nod and a "How are you?" The lady looked at me suspiciously and immediately proceeded to another aisle.

Then, it dawned on me that these neighborhood folks weren't that neighborly, and apparently they were just here to shop. Can you believe that? Plus, that was the first Walmart I've ever visited that didn't have WD-40 and deer corn for sale.

Back home in my small-town Walmart, I would be greeted by people entering and exiting the wrong doors, worn out buggies, narrow, overcrowded aisles, and lines backed up waiting for an available checker. I would see many people I knew, would be questioned about the Cubs 2020 chances, asked about my grandchildren, and teased about being the Walmart guy. And, at my Walmart, if I stood at the front of the store with a buggy filled with groceries, a nice employee would walk up and ask if she could check me out in the self-checkout lane.

Now that is a "Neighborhood Market." And, we always have deer corn!

Chapter 37

A Year of Stories ...

It has been one year since I wrote the first "Dear Walmart" note of frustration. I wrote that short letter as self-prescribed therapy after a brief verbal exchange with an employee who obviously had never heard of Sam Walton. Since then, I have made over 100 trips to our local store and I stand by the statement I made in Chapter 5: "There is no such thing as an uneventful trip to Walmart."

In the past year, my shopping skills have improved greatly. I know my way around the fruits and vegetables section. I check the dates on arugula. I know how to select the best papaya, the best asparagus, and I can open those little plastic bags while holding three mangoes. My greatest talent is selecting the best hickory smoked ham, even if it means digging to the bottom of the pile. I'm still no expert, but I move through the store with a confident fluidity that did not exist a year ago. At my age, maybe fluidity is a stretch, but at least I'm no longer stumbling around all over the store looking for every item on my list.

I no longer dread Walmart trips; in fact, I look forward to the challenge. I find great pleasure in completing a shopping list. Every time I place an item in the cart, I get a warm feeling of accomplishment. In my mind, a shopping list is like a football schedule and as I conquer the eggs and place them in the victory cart, I immediately begin to think about my next opponent. As soon as the milk is defeated and laid to rest, my eyes are focused on the cheese, then the cereal, then the chips ... well, you get the picture. As each opponent is defeated, I place a "W" by their name and move closer to the finish line. Some opponents are more difficult than others, so I really must get mentally ready to take on the grapes and the celery. I have lost more than I've won when it comes to celery. I am always happy as I steer a full cart of defeated opponents into victory lane. Okay, I will go ahead and say it ... I've lost my mind! I enjoy grocery shopping at Walmart.

With those words, I guess it may be time to find another topic to write about. I'm just not as upset with Walmart as I was a year ago. Truthfully, writing about Walmart does seem a little weird for a retired minister and it seems that none of the changes I've recommended have been taken seriously. Plus, I really don't want these Walmart Words to be my legacy, but it may be too late for that.

Not long ago, after preaching a stirring message in a small church, an elderly lady "walked the aisle" during the invitation. I greeted her and asked how I could help. She whispered that she had to leave early, but did not want to leave without telling me how much she loved my Walmart stories. I am not kidding. She said nothing about my sermon. Thank you, Walmart, for changing my life purpose and my legacy. May all your entrance doors be broken. I'm checking out.

Book Two
_____

Just Saying

Chapter 1

A Trashy Tale

There are two kinds of people in the world—those who are saved and those who throw trash out of their vehicle.

A few days ago, I spent a couple of hours picking up trash from the side of the road leading to our house ... two 30-gallon trash bags jammed full of cans, bottles, plastic bags, tobacco cans, cigarette packages, empty food containers, Styrofoam drink cups, and one pregnancy test.

Congratulations!

We love where we live, and the steep, winding, uphill road that leads to our driveway should be a scenic and serene trip, but its peaceful effect is trashed when inconsiderate humans can't think of a better way to get rid of their trash than by throwing it out the window. Here's a brilliant idea: you know that plastic bag they put your Sprite in or that container in your lap as you eat your chicken? Put your filthy trash in that and take it to your own trash can, or, if you don't want your family seeing your empty bottles or your pregnancy test, there are trash cans at every gas station in our community. Surely there are better options than throwing trash from a moving vehicle into God's front yard.

I'm not sure I will be often motivated to pick up the trash on our uphill road. I don't know the exact distance from the main highway to our mailbox, but I do know that it's 664 uphill steps and that the ditches on both sides of our road are steep, at least for my 70-plus-year-old knees. I had taken precautions by wearing my orange hunting vest and orange Farm Bureau cap, and I had my green Gator Grabber in one hand and the black garbage bag in the other. Charlotte asked that I wear a face mask to conceal my identity, but at this stage of life, I have no pride left. Occasionally, the county will use incarcerated men in white clothing to pick up roadside trash, but I looked more like an escapee from a Nursing Home Halloween party.

Walking back up our hill, I had flashbacks of running wind sprints with legs burning and lungs crying out for air. I stopped once to catch my breath and almost tumbled over backwards. "Must. Keep. Moving. Forward," I said, as I gasped for more air. I finally made it to our house where my loving wife greeted me with these kind words, "Don't ever do that again." I took her words to heart.

I'm considering purchasing a goat for roadside clean-up. I could put him on a leash and take him for a walk and he could eat trash to his heart's content. I could put up some of those "Men Working" signs at the bottom and top of our hill, except my signs would say, "GNAW" … Goat Now At Work. When my goat has finished gnawing his way to the bottom of the hill, I could ride him back up the hill and save my knees for easier chores around the house. I'm just saying that a better idea would be for everyone to stop throwing your filthy trash out of your vehicles.

That's just Baaaaaaadd!!

Chapter 2

Influence of Music

As I sat in church Sunday morning, I began to think about how much my life has been influenced by music...especially Christian music. I don't sing well, I don't read music, I don't play a musical instrument, and I don't know the difference between a falsetto and a muffaletta, but music seems to stir up emotions and memories like nothing else I know. I can't even write about it without crying.

Forty years ago I heard an elderly Christian man sing a song entitled, "The Longer I Serve Him, The Sweeter He Grows." Time had done a number on his voice (pun intended), and he couldn't sing very well, but the words were coming from his heart after years of walking with God. Forty years later, in my mind, I can still hear his voice, and those words.

My dad, who did have a nice voice, loved to attend church "singings," which were normally held on Sunday afternoons in a nearby host church. He would always take me with him, and we would listen to different individuals or groups "bring the special music." Honestly, most of it wasn't too special, but I would give anything to be able to sit next to him just one more time and watch him cry to the words of, "The Old Rugged Cross." He would cry every time it was sung; it didn't matter who was singing it. His lip would start quivering, just like mine is right now, and tears would stream down his face, and he would gently shake his head back and forth like he was trying to silently apologize. No apologies needed, Dad!

I grew up attending a small, country church that sang out of a "shape note" hymnal. I don't even know what that means except that all the squiggles above and below the words were different from other squiggles in other hymnals. Our church also believed in extending an invitation at the conclusion of every worship service. Before I committed my life to Christ, I always dreaded the invitation song. The words of some of those songs would seem to single me out and overwhelm me with conviction about my need for salvation. I always dreaded Sunday nights when we would sing, "O, why not tonight? Wilt thou be saved? Then, why not tonight?" I would hold on to the back of the wooden pew in front of me until my knuckles were white, but I would not "walk the aisle". During one summer revival, I let go of that pew and received Jesus as my Savior as the church was singing, "Oh, happy day, oh, happy day, when Jesus washed my sins away." It was indeed a happy day.

I have been blessed to worship with Jesus-followers all over the world and to hear them making joyful noises to the Lord in languages that I could not understand, although I completely understood their hearts. While traveling in Russia, I met some young Christians from Tanzania who were the only Christians in their village. To avoid persecution, they went some distance away from the village, dug a deep hole, and climbed down into the hole so they could sing and not be heard by those who might harm them. I asked them to sing their favorite song, and they began singing their own version of "I was glad when they said, 'Let us go into the house of the Lord.'" I could not speak. In China, I was moved to tears as believers would "whisper sing" so that neighbors could not hear and report them to the Communist authorities. It was humbling.

It's not just the old hymns that move me. Not long ago at our church, our youth sang Chris Tomlin's song, "Is He Worthy?" Listening to those young voices singing those beautiful words moved me so deeply that I could not fight back the tears. Believe me, I tried. The tears just continued to stream down my face, and I lifted my hand in the air believing that it would somehow communicate more vividly what I wanted to say to God in that moment. That is not a common act of worship for me, but in that moment, to not raise my hand in worship would have been disobedience.

Unlike some in my generation, I love contemporary Christian music, and in my opinion, the songs just keep getting better. If it's Scriptural, if it directs me to focus on God, if it honors His Son, and if it calls me to love Him, then it's probably going to make my lip quiver. I love to sing and I'm glad you don't have to be good at it to make a noise that pleases the Lord.

I'm just saying that we should appreciate the freedoms we have and that we should sing until our lips quiver and tears stream down our face. No apologies needed.

Chapter 3

Church Weathervane

I was "called to preach" at First Baptist Church in Hope, Arkansas. I was also privileged to pastor my home church for nine years. It is a beautiful church building, constructed in the late 1940s with the kind of handiwork we don't see anymore and couldn't afford to duplicate. One interesting thing about the building is that on top of the high steeple is a weathervane. Not a cross or a spire, but a weathervane.

One day my office phone rang, and it was a dear friend who had grown up in Hope and worked at a downtown business. He said, "Stan, I'm sitting here looking out my office window and I just noticed that your church has a weathervane on top of the steeple. Why a weathervane?" I was too embarrassed to admit to him that I had never noticed that either, but I said to him without hesitating, "It's to remind our community that no matter which way the wind is blowing, God is still God and there is always hope." I have no idea why our predecessors chose to put a weathervane on top of the steeple, but I'm sticking to my explanation. Since we are living in such a cloud of uncertainty, it is calming to remember those things of which we are certain. I am certain that it does not matter what the crisis may be, God is still God and there is hope.

This morning I stood at our front window for a long time watching a flock of robins in our yard. Being a counter, I counted 17. They did not seem worried or overly anxious about anything.

It was very peaceful watching them hop around feeding off of the delicacies found in there. It was also reassuring to remember that God sees each bird and knows when each one hops. *"Look at the birds of the air, that they do not sow, nor reap nor gather into barns, and yet your heavenly Father feeds them. Are you not worth much more than they?"* (Matthew 6:26 NASB)

We will all learn things from this pandemic. I have already learned that I touch my face a lot, especially my nose. I have also learned that it's very difficult to floss without touching your face. I have learned that a "must have" item on my quarantine list is Dot's pretzels found at Atwoods. Also, it was not good timing for our state newspaper to have stopped its daily deliveries. These iPads are good for reading the news, but cannot be used as a replacement for emergency toilet paper.

I have also learned not only the importance of washing my hands more often, but also the importance of folding my hands more often in prayer. Both the washing and the praying are crucial for our situation. My plan has become, "I'm taking this seriously, and praying fervently."

I'm just saying that our nation has a history of enduring strong and strange winds from all directions, and nothing has ever changed the fact that God is still God and there is always hope.

Chapter 4

Walking by Faith

Our dog is losing his eyesight. Cubbie will soon be 13 years old and neither Charlotte nor I will even discuss what we will do when he is no longer with us. He's been a great dog, and it's painful to watch him as he adjusts to the limitations that go with being older. He probably feels the same way about us.

I remember when we first saw him. The owners placed four or five adorable Corgi puppies on the ground, and he took off running as fast as he could for the gate to freedom. We knew it might be risky, but we chose him on the spot. That was only the beginning of his exploring runs to what he thought would be freedom. Those escapes often led to danger, but he seemed to mature with age and now he stays close to home.

Since his eyesight became an issue, we've noticed several changes in his behavior. I have always taken him out at night just before bedtime and he knows the routine. All I have to do is head for the door with the flashlight and he darts to the door, takes two steps outside, takes off running, and starts barking. We have followed that routine thousands of times through the years. The last couple of nights, he has taken those two steps, stopped, and looked back at me over his shoulder. I have simply said, "It's okay, buddy, I'm going with you." He stays close. He still barks. He still sniffs. But he is always looking back over his shoulder to find me. He trusts me, and I am always standing there for him. It's almost like he's walking by faith and not by sight. Interesting, isn't it?

Right now, we are certainly being called upon to walk by faith, and we certainly can trust the Master. He has promised *"I will never desert you, nor will I ever forsake you,"* (Hebrews 13:5 NASB). *"God is our refuge and strength, A very present help in trouble."* (Psalms 46:1 NASB)

Perhaps, through the years, some of us have taken some of those escape runs through what we thought was a door to more freedom, only to find ourselves in great danger. Hopefully, we have matured enough to find our way back home. Home means staying close to the Master. In these uncertain days, it may seem dark, and it might get darker, but He who is the Light is saying, "It's okay, I am going with you."

I'm just saying that during these days of at-home quarantine, just make sure you're staying close to the Master. The promises of His presence should provide all the reassurance we need.

Chapter 5

Funerals and Easter

We have had our share of funerals in the past few months. It's always good to see our church family respond in such a kind and caring way to those who are mourning. In fact, it's one of the things our church does best. We genuinely grieve with those who are grieving and we continue to walk with them as they adjust to a new phase of life. Thank you for being that kind of loving church family.

There is no greater honor given to those of us in ministry than to be asked by a family to speak at the memorial service of their deceased family member. Even though I have spoken at hundreds of funerals, I have never really gotten comfortable with that responsibility. I am always nervous and it is the most emotionally draining thing I do in ministry. I have always seen my role as honoring the life of the deceased while at the same time honoring the Lord. I always pray that the family and the people attending will experience the presence of God in an overwhelming way.

I remember one of the first funerals I "preached" in my first pastorate. I was asked by the local funeral home to officiate a graveside service for a local man who had no church home and no pastor. I met the funeral director and his assistant at the graveside and we were the only three in attendance. A slow rain began to fall and the director asked me if I would just say a prayer. I started to pray and I started to cry. I could not believe that this man had no family, no friends, and not one person to attend his funeral. I began to pray that if there was anyone else in that town who was alone in life that we might find them and befriend them and tell them about Jesus. The longer I prayed, the more I cried, and the harder it rained. Finally, the director just touched me on the arm and said, "Preacher, you've done a good job."

One positive thing about Christian funerals ... they always end with a word of hope. We know we have not seen the last of our loved ones. We believe that they are not dead, but alive and in the presence of Jesus. For the follower of Jesus, death is just the entrance into an eternity filled with peace, joy, and the presence of God.

Easter is the Christian's celebration of death's defeat!! Jesus died and rose again. He defeated death and took the fear away. He made a way for us to be absent from these bodies and to be present with God. Easter is a reminder that we, too, will be resurrected and reunited with our loved ones in heaven. Easter allows us to mourn our loved ones in a healthy way and never be overwhelmed because of our temporary separation.

We miss them, but we shall see them again.

Chapter 6

Dealing with Loss

There are times that I write because I feel there is a message or a truth that needs to be shared. There are other times that I write because people need to laugh, or reminisce, or reflect. Today, I am writing because I am selfish, and I am having a difficult time dealing with the death of a longtime friend. I just need to emotionally exhale, and writing enables me to do that in a semi-private and more peaceful way.

Don't judge me, please. I am a follower of Jesus and a pastor with a missionary heart. I know the theological truths about the "departure" of a Christian and I believe those truths of Scripture. I have proclaimed them for forty-six years at hundreds of funerals and gravesides. My friend was a Christian. He and I had that discussion several years ago. I am confident that he is in heaven and that he is perfectly healed from the debilitating disease that ended his earthly life. He's okay, and I know that, but I'm not as okay as I know I should be.

He and I were teammates in college and there we became close friends. We were both married at about the same time, had our first child at about the same time, and entered the coaching profession at the same time. We have remained close through the years, and he loved me as a friend before and after I was committed to Christ.

He was the toughest guy I have ever known. He really did not know how strong he was. His quick temper matched his red hair and to say that he had a short fuse would be like saying that Walmart has a few groceries. He also had a heart as big as his home state of Texas. Those players whom he coached all know about his toughness and most of them know personally of his generosity. You wanted him on your side and once he was on your side, you had a genuine friend.

I've lost friends before, so why is this one so different? I don't know. That's why I'm writing. Maybe it's because there can be no public celebration of his life … no closure, like we've grown accustomed to with our cultural funeral services. Maybe it's because I can't get in the car and drive to his home and verbally express my condolences to his wife and children. Maybe it's because I can't hug anybody, especially my other teammates who always show up in times like this. I cherish those hugs. Maybe it's because he and I shared so much and laughed so much and cared so much. Maybe it's because I wish that we had spent more time together in recent years and the fact that we really, really don't know when we will be seeing each other for the last time on earth.

I'll be fine. This is selfish. This Sunday is Easter!! My friend is getting all the hugs he needs from the Resurrected Lord. I will see him again and he will be among the first I will hug. I'm just saying that when I see some of you, and can, I'm probably gonna hug you.

Chapter 7

Time to Mind-Travel

Being self-quarantined for four weeks gives you an abundance of time to mind-travel. I have enjoyed sitting on our back patio listening to the sounds, watching the birds and the butterflies, and just taking in the beauty of the Lord's creation. Being a man human, I can sit for long periods of time without thinking about anything. Honestly! Charlotte doesn't believe that to be possible, but I truly can sit for a very long time without any noticeable brain activity. Charlotte walks up to me and says, "What are you thinking about?" I look her in the eyes and answer honestly, "Absolutely nothing."

However, during the lock down, I have been thinking about a lot of things. For example, the best cup of coffee I've ever had was in the airport in Maracaibo, Venezuela. There's not even a close second. Those guys make a cafe con leche that will make you want to miss your flight.

The best plate of rice I've ever eaten was in a Turkish restaurant in Istanbul. The worst was on an island in the Maldives. We were eating with our hands and the food was so hot it made my eyes water. Did I mention that we were eating with our hands!!?? A close second to the worst was in the Lunchroom at Paisley Elementary School on West Avenue B in Hope, Arkansas. The Thursday lunch menu called it "Spanish Rice," but that's not we were calling it at the fourth grade table. I took my half-empty plate to the dish pit, but I was stopped by one of the teachers. She told me to go back to my seat and eat the rest of that rice. I did, and then barfed up the Thursday menu in the large trash can.

Paisley Elementary provided a well-rounded education for its students, and I'm not even talking about the classrooms. There were frequent fights on the playground and in the bathrooms. One of our sixth graders actually drove a car to school. Baseball records were legendary, and each grade had their contender for the coveted Most Broken Windows award. Hyperactive students were not given medication, but tied into their desks with a safety-patrol belt. Recesses almost always ended with torn clothing and/or bloody noses. I loved that school.

My first-grade teacher, Miss Caldwell, would allow me to sit in her lap during naptime because I would "tear up" thinking about and missing my parents. I did not have the benefit of attending kindergarten, so this was my first time to be away from my parents. Mrs. Adams, our sixth-grade teacher, used a wooden boat paddle to keep order. Mrs. Copeland used her hand on the backside of our britches. The thing I loved most about Paisley was that when warm weather came, we could take our shoes off after lunch and go barefooted the rest of the day. Luckily, I still had my shoes on the day I threw up "un montón de" Spanish rice. It's amazing what comes to mind when we have so much time to mind-travel.

Mostly, during these quiet days, I've been thinking about how much my faith in Christ means to me. The thought of a worldwide pandemic should bring us to the place of acknowledging our own mortality. I'm not being morbid, just real. Perhaps this invisible enemy, or virus, invaded our comfortable and complacent lifestyles at just the right time. Our eyes have been opened to how frail and fragile life on earth really is. Hopefully, we also have come to the realization of real priorities. I miss people. I miss family. I miss fellowship. I miss corporate worship. Some things that I have held onto as important necessities have been sidelined for a while, and I'm amazed at how little they are missed.

I'm thankful for good memories, the grace of a loving Lord, and a new grasp of what's important. I'm thankful that social distancing does not mean spiritual distancing. I'm thankful that our relationship with Christ means that nothing will ever separate us from the Father. I'm just saying that we may never have another extended period like this to reflect on what really matters most.

(By the way, Paisley rules!)

Chapter 8

Quality Time

One of the first observations I made when I retired six years ago was not only should you love your wife, but you need to make sure that you like her. It also helps if she likes you, because spending quality time together has not been an issue since 11:38 a.m., March 14, 2020, when we made the decision to self-quarantine.

Since that decision was made, we have only been apart for the few minutes it takes me to drive to Grocery Pick-up, to the Pharmacy Drive Through, and to the Post Office drop box. There have been moments when Charlotte has suggested that I "don't have to hurry back," or maybe I should drive out to the dam and check the water level at the lake. We've lived here for 12 years, and she's never been interested in the lake.

The male/female differences and our personality differences seem to have been exacerbated during our lockdown. I could list several examples, but there is one glaring difference that has become extremely obvious. My wife has the ability to multitask, and I am a "limited tasker." I can "task," but not very fast and only one task at a time. Charlotte can play an advanced word game on her phone while watching a British documentary as she prepares a four-course meal and talks to me about what we need to plant in the garden. On the other hand, I like to watch Hallmark movies and I have to stay focused on the plot or I get confused.

Communication has become an issue, or maybe it's my hearing loss because I can only hear one thing at a time. I do not have the ability to listen to and intelligently participate in three or four conversations at one time. My super-tasking wife can do that while riding a bicycle across a tightrope and at the same time ordering the QVC Today's Special Value. I feel extremely inferior and limited. I can hear her, but I never know which conversation we're having. I'm focused on the exciting movie and that's all my brain can compute at one time. The pause button on the remote is worn smooth. In the last seven weeks, I have answered, "I agree," to hundreds of things about which I have no clue.

I'm just saying that it's great to love your wife, even better to like her, and essential that you trust her. If you agree, just nod your head, and focus on the television.

Chapter 9

The Power of a Spatula

Charlotte and I celebrated our 50th wedding anniversary in 2019 and we are both aware that it is a shared commitment to Christ that has both "glued" and held us together.

We are very different in so many ways, perhaps like a lot of other couples.

We met in college. She was an English major who was serious about her courses, and I was in college too. She loved art, pottery making, dance, reading, and studying. I played football and majored in interceptions. Our first date was an accident and a disaster, but the second was by design, and enjoyable. We were married our junior year. I have asked her several times through the years why she agreed to go out with me a second time and her response has always been the same ... "I really don't know."

I have often shared that our marriage began to change in year five when I read 1 Peter 3:7, *"Likewise, husbands, live with your wives in an understanding way ..."* All jokes aside about "you'll never understand her," my take on that verse was, and still is, to understand what I must do to become the husband she needs me to be. For me, that involved a spiritual transformation and a lot of retraining for my "only child" mindset.

So, over the course of these past years, we have been able to find and share mutual interests and activities, despite our differences. She became a baseball fan, so I became interested in bird watching. She tried and liked deer meat, so I watched

Masterpiece Theater. She will watch the Bourne Movies with me, so I will watch *Pride and Prejudice*. She loves to work in the yard, so I … well, I'm still trying to love that.

When I retired in 2016, I started cooking our breakfast every morning. Charlotte is a wonderful cook, so I became her trainee in the kitchen. My idea of cooking was crackers and cheese with a milkshake. She now brags on my perfect eggs and I'm happy to make her happy.

Today, I said to her, "What does it mean that I have a favorite spatula?" A look of peaceful contentment spread across her sweet face and a smile that reached into her eyes. That was the look of peace, safety, and security that I have longed to see in my wife's face. After 50 years of marriage, I learned that the secret was a spatula! A spatula!! I could have avoided the birds, PBS, and all chick flicks if I had just known the power of a spatula.

I'm just saying that Saint Peter should have elaborated and explained that a spatula can "turn" your marriage around.

Chapter 10

Pay Attention to Blue Jays

I have mentioned before that Charlotte is an avid bird watcher, and although not at her level, I also enjoy watching and listening while sitting on our patio. The early morning bird symphony coming from the woods surrounding our house is incredible. At certain times of the day, our bird feeders are as busy as the drive-through at our community's new Taco Bell. My favorite bird is the Summer Tanager. The strawberry-colored male is completely red, and not cardinal red, which is great because I am a Cubs fan. The female Tanager is an impressive yellow-green, which means that opposites do attract, even in bird world. You can learn a lot while watching birds.

My least favorite is the Blue Jay who, just by his sheer size, is a bully around the feeders. However, when you live in the country, especially this time of year, this bird becomes a much needed and welcomed alarm system at the first sign of a snake. We have learned not to avoid, but rather to pay careful attention to the danger call of a Blue Jay. Anytime we hear that warning call, we stop what we're doing in order to investigate, and we walk cautiously.

So, I've just told you everything I know about bird world, but with all this extra time to think, observe, and reflect, my bird-brain has been flying in circles. It seems that the warning call of the Blue Jay is very similar to my conscience. It warns me of danger and when I hear it, I should stop what I'm getting ready to do, investigate, and walk cautiously. I've also noticed that when I am not tuned in to the Blue Jay's warnings, I can find myself much closer to danger than I need to be. If I continuously ignore his warning call, I can actually tune it out completely, very similar to the gradual hardening of a calloused conscience. I pay attention to Blue Jays, but many times, I've refused to pay attention to my inner alert system, the one placed there by God to keep me from harm, and it has not turned out well.

Many people in the past few months have posted and referred us to 2nd Chronicles 7:12-14. Read it carefully. Read it contextually. God says to His people, those who are called by His name, that when we look around and see the sad condition of our land, we are to make the connection to the condition of our own hearts. In other words, we cannot continue to ignore and tune out the squawking Blue Jays that are telling us to stop, investigate our decisions, and turn around before we walk into danger. If I examine my own conscience, and confess my own sin, and turn toward and seek God, and if you also make that decision … well, "birds of a feather flock together."

I'm just saying that we would all be better off if we listened more intently to warnings and stopped to investigate before we take steps. Any birdbrain should understand that.

Chapter 11

Our Real Hope

Hy·poc·ri·sy /h päkr s /—noun—*the practice of claiming to have moral standards or beliefs to which one's own behavior does not conform; pretense.*

Hate /h t/—verb—*feel intense or passionate dislike for (someone).*

Hope /h p/—noun—*a feeling of expectation and desire for a certain thing to happen.*

Regardless of where you stand and regardless of personal perspective, surely you will agree that we are seeing plenty of hypocrisy, plenty of hate, and not much real hope.

"Hope" is commonly used to mean a wish: its strength is the strength of the person's desire. But in the Bible, "hope" is the confident expectation of what God has promised and its strength is in His faithfulness. Biblical hope is our only hope. We cannot just strongly wish that our situation gets better and expect any positive changes. Hope based on anything or anyone other than God and His faithfulness can do nothing to deter hypocrisy or hate.

In my opinion, that is where we, the church, have failed. We have failed to share the Gospel in the power of the Holy Spirit and for this we are all guilty. Our cities, big and small, are void of Spirit-filled followers of Christ, who have the only true remedy to the deadly "H" viruses of hypocrisy, hatred, and false hope. What have we been doing? According to John 15:5, nothing of eternal value. Look it up and read it.

I grew up just outside of Hope, Arkansas. That's the way my father always told people where we lived ... "just outside of Hope." I'm in the process of writing a book (who isn't), and that's the title, "Just Outside of Hope." The book is not about growing up in a place called Hope, but rather it's about people who thought they were beyond hope, and some who did not know that hope was even a possibility, and yet, their situations were not hopeless. The truth is they were just outside of hope, but closer than they ever imagined.

That's where we are as a nation, and those of us who claim to be Jesus' disciples must take Spirit-led steps to unleash the supernatural, life-changing, redeeming power of the Truth of the Gospel. I'm just saying, that is, always has been, and forever will be our only real hope. Many will deny, reject, and refuse to submit to the Truth of Jesus. That is their choice, but the cure is too lifesaving not to share.

"But what does it say? "THE WORD IS NEAR YOU, IN YOUR MOUTH AND IN YOUR HEART"—that is, the word of faith which we are preaching, that if you confess with your mouth Jesus as Lord, and believe in your heart that God raised Him from the dead, you will be saved; for with the heart a person believes, resulting in righteousness, and with the mouth he confesses, resulting in salvation. For the Scripture says, "WHOEVER BELIEVES IN HIM WILL NOT BE DISAPPOINTED." For there is no distinction between Jew and Greek; for the same Lord is Lord of all, abounding in riches for all who call on Him; for "WHOEVER WILL CALL ON THE NAME OF THE LORD WILL BE SAVED." How then will they call on Him in whom they have not believed? How will they believe in Him whom they have not heard? And how will they hear without a preacher? How will they preach unless they are sent? Just as it is written, "HOW BEAUTIFUL ARE THE

FEET OF THOSE WHO BRING GOOD NEWS OF GOOD THINGS!" (Romans 10:8-15 NASB)

By the way, being controlled by the Holy Spirit replaces hypocrisy, hatred, and hopelessness with holiness. Just saying.

Chapter 12

Keep the Rivers Flowing

A few years ago, the culvert that drains water from our front yard to the other side of the road was squashed. When I say squashed, I mean flattened like stomping on an empty can. Therefore, the water that once flowed from our yard has no place to flow, so instead of flowing it now settles and becomes what we call, "Lake Parris." We do not want a lake in our front yard.

A few days ago, a friend showed up with his backhoe and un-squashed the flattened culvert. So, I began to shovel out the mud, sludge, and debris that had accumulated in the blocked culvert. I soon learned three things about the dilemma: 1) I'm too old to clean out culverts. 2) When a culvert is blocked, it creates a lot of debris. Now, we're waiting on the next rain to see if the water will flow or if more debris will need to be removed.

While I was shoveling, I kept thinking about the words of Jesus recorded in John 7: *"Now on the last day, the great day of the feast, Jesus stood and cried out, saying, "If anyone is thirsty, let him come to Me and drink. He who believes in Me, as the Scripture said, 'From his innermost being will flow rivers of living water.'" But this He spoke of the Spirit, whom those who believed in Him were to receive; for the Spirit was not yet given, because Jesus was not yet glorified."* (John 7:37-39 NASB)

Being a Christian and a preacher, those kind of thoughts come to me often, but honestly, when they do I know they're from the Lord. Most of my thoughts while shoveling were about the idiot or idiots who kept running off the road smashing our beloved culvert. So, when the "flowing rivers of living water" image came, I knew it was from the Lord and I knew that it was not only for me, but also about me.

As a follower of Jesus, I believe that He lives in me in the person of the Holy Spirit. That's what the passage in John is all about. His life is to flow through me, but all kinds of debris in my life can stop the flow and when that happens things get messy. I must keep the channel clean so the Life can flow.

Oh, and the third thing I learned through this dilemma: 3) Debris causes damage. Because of the clogged-up culvert in front of our house, a lot of damage has been done to the road, the front-end alignment on many cars driving down our road, and was the cause of at least one blown tire. The longer the culvert was damaged the more damage it caused to others, therefore, my debris most definitely affects the lives of others.

So, as I was shoveling and sweating, I came to an agreement with the Lord that I would take extra precautions to keep the debris cleared and the life flowing. I'm just saying that I don't want to contribute to the damage, but rather, I want "the rivers of living water flowing from my innermost being." Keep shoveling.

Chapter 13

Getting Older

As the nice young man placed my groceries in the back seat of my truck, our conversation turned to spiritual matters. He listened intently, probably because it's hard to hear someone speaking through a mask while social distancing, but he was listening. I did not mind that he shuffled closer to my window as the topic gravitated toward the sovereignty of God and His faithfulness. After a few more minutes of conversation, he smiled through his mask and said, "I always enjoy talking to the elderly."

Okay, I'm old! But as the saying goes, "Don't worry about getting old, worry about thinking old." My problem is not thinking old; my problem is that my thinker is old. Apparently, I have gained so much knowledge, wisdom, and experience through these many years that my thinker is running out of room. I'm pretty sure I have used up valuable space just trying to remember passwords. These days I can remember much better than I can think. What I mean is, I can remember things that occurred over 60 years ago, but I can't think as fast on my feet as I could just a few years ago. Charlotte says, "What are you thinking about?" My response, "I'm not thinking, I'm remembering." I'm much better at remembering. I think that means I'm getting old, and I'm not sure I like it, but all the signs are there.

For example, it seems the globe is spinning faster, and the changes are changing before I can adjust to what just changed. I'm not opposed to change that is sensible, efficient, and beneficial, but nobody checks with me and gets my opinion about said changes. I don't remember things changing as quickly or maybe my thinker has just run out of space to compute any more changes.

And then there's this … a few years ago I was standing much higher on a ladder than I should have been. As the ladder began to fall, I remembered all the drills I had repeated countless times in my athletic days. Drills that taught me how to fall, roll, and protect myself. My thinker kicked into action as the ladder was falling and I kept waiting for the signals to spring me into roll and protect action. I disengaged from the ladder with perfect timing, but all those athletic skills had been lost somewhere in the past. That day I learned that I don't roll anymore; all I do is fall, and I have even lost the ability to do that gracefully. My thinker must have been counting on muscle memory to kick in. What was my thinker thinking? My muscles are in worse shape than my memory!

Frequently, I find myself saying, "If I've already told you this, just stop me." If you have as much information stored away in your thinker as most 73-year-olds, you shouldn't have to be held accountable for not remembering if you've already said something. You should be congratulated for remembering that you have something to say. In my opinion, my stories are like my sermons, if they're worth sharing once then they're worth repeating.

I'm just saying that admitting you're getting old is better than worrying about it. I'm not worried about getting old, and my thinking is not old, it's just tired. I think I'll just trust the sovereignty of God and His faithfulness.

Chapter 14

New Car Phobia

I learned to drive in my dad's 1955 Ford. It had an eight-cylinder engine with a three-speed transmission and the gearshift was on the column. I would sit in the parked vehicle and practice shifting gears while making the sounds of the engine as I ran through the gears.

I started driving when I was 10. My dad would let me drive by myself down the gravel road to Long's Store to get bread and milk. I would always "spin out" on the loose gravel and speed shift from first to second gear. I could barely see over the steering wheel.

When I was in the seventh grade, my dad let me take our 1960 Rambler to the homecoming dance. Even crazier were the parents of the seventh grade girl who allowed their daughter to go with me. As a ninth grader with a learner's permit, I was driving home after baseball practice when I saw a State Police roadblock several blocks ahead. I did a quick U-turn and headed for a back road to avoid the roadblock. The trooper saw my attempt to avoid him and quickly jumped in his car to pull me over. He walked up to my window, asked to see my license, and said, "Does your dad know that you're driving this car?" "Yes sir," I said. "Well, you'd better get home. Be careful."

All of this to say that I have been driving for a long time and have experience with all kinds of vehicles. But we recently purchased a new car (actually a pre-owned car) and I'm scared to death of it. This car doesn't even have a key. I can't find the battery.

126

It keeps asking how it can help me. The owner's manual is 272 pages and is written in an unknown language. I read the words, but have no idea what they are describing. For example, the Driver Information Display (DID) is located in the "instrument cluster." The manual says to scroll up for menus, scroll down for submenus, or scroll right to access the information screens or submenu screens of a main menu item. I pushed the okay button and it said I had reset all displayed features that can be reset. I was just trying to see how fast I was going. Who writes these manuals? When did driving become so complicated?

The control panel (instrument cluster) has more lights than my mother's Christmas tree. I thought I was adjusting the volume on the radio, but instead hit something called the Auto Stick Gear Paddle. All of a sudden, our six-cylinder car sounded like that 1955 Ford in first gear … but I couldn't find a clutch. I pulled over, prayed, and told Siri that I was not praying to her. The radio volume will remain at twelve for as long as we have this car. I'm afraid to adjust it.

It's a very nice car, but how much technology do we really need and how much help is helpful? Do I really need six different settings for my windshield wipers? There are sixteen buttons that control the radio. It can also be voice activated by speaking into the rear-view mirror. Which, by the way, I am afraid to adjust because it has a red 911 emergency button right where your hand goes. I have only adjusted the side view mirrors, but that was after I mistakenly hit the seat warmer button, which, by the way, automatically comes on in the high hot setting. I did find the fuel-filler door button that opens the fuel-filler door, but there was no gas cap, just a fuel flapper … whatever. At least I wasn't looking for the gas cap behind the license plate … remember that? We will eventually learn everything we need to know about our car, but I'm sure there are features we will never use or even know we have. It's a very nice car.

I'm just saying that I would have been very hesitant to have gone to the seventh grade homecoming dance in a car that doesn't have a key or a gas cap, and yet, is so intimidating. I kind of miss cars that are so easy to drive that even a 10-year-old can speed shift on a gravel road.

Chapter 15

Peaceful Tears

One of the reasons I enjoy writing is to make people laugh. We need to laugh. Those of you who knew my dad probably remember that he loved to laugh, and it didn't take much to get him started. One of my uncles was a master storyteller and every time we visited him, my dad would have tears in his eyes from laughter. I loved going to his house. It was comforting to hear Dad's laughter. *"A joyful heart makes a cheerful face, but when the heart is sad, the spirit is broken."* (Proverbs 15:13 NASB)

The Bible also states that there is a time to cry, and that, too, can be comforting. I understand laughter a lot more than I understand crying. Our Venezuelan friends say that God gives us tears so that our heads will not get too big. That's a great thought, but probably not a universal explanation for all our tears.

My crying is so random, unpredictable, and haphazard. As minister, I have experienced all kinds of tragic, terrible, and traumatic situations. In most cases, God has enabled me to remain calm and peaceful, and, at times, has given me the right words for the moment. But there have been other moments when I really needed to hold it together, needed to maintain composure, needed to control my emotions, and those random, unpredictable, and haphazard tears would show up and stream down my face. I have no explanation.

Of course, the older I get the more random and unpredictable my tears become. I cry at the oddest moments. I cry when

I'm alone. I cry when a favorite song comes on the radio. I cry when I watch *Rudy*, and *Hoosiers*, and *Sergeant York*, even though I have seen those movies dozens and dozens of times. I don't cry at the end of Hallmark movies, except for that one where the country-western singer sings, "Sometimes a cowboy rides away, sometimes he rides back home to stay." And then, he marries his childhood sweetheart in the loft of a barn. See what I mean … who cries over a barn wedding?

Certain sights, sounds, and smells can trigger those unpredictable tears. The smell of freshly cut grass on an August morning brings back memories of football practices, which I hated at the time, but which now stir up good thoughts of good friends. Some of those friends have passed away, but have not passed out of my memory. Who cries over wet grass? It's embarrassing.

I recently finished watching a 96-episode Spanish language novella on Netflix. It was produced in Colombia and everything about it was familiar and brought back images, moments, and memories that I treasure. I would pause the movie just to take in everything on the screen. I could smell the food carts, hear the buses, and recognize almost everything in the houses. I would think, "I know these people, I love these people, I miss these people" … and the tears would flow. By the way, you know nothing about binging until you have lived through a Spanish language novella.

My favorite time of day is what Chicago Cubs radio announcer Pat Hughes calls "twilight." By definition, it's that time of day "in which the atmosphere is partially illuminated by the sun, being neither totally dark or completely lit." Nostalgia envelopes me at twilight time and I often gravitate outside to the front porch or to our driveway. I remember driving home after football, basketball, track, or baseball practice and seeing the lights coming on as people arrived home from work. I would arrive home and walk into a warm kitchen, the sound of the pressure cooker on the stove, and the smell of butter beans and cornbread. My mother would be busily moving around in our small kitchen and would almost always say, "Supper is about ready." For me, twilight is associated with going home.

Twilight is also defined as "a period of obscurity, ambiguity, or gradual decline … he was in the twilight of his career." Please don't be concerned about my mental or emotional state, it's just that I get teary-eyed thinking about this fourth quarter of life and the time I have left before going home. These are not sad tears, or fearful tears, or remorseful tears; these are thankful tears and grateful tears. Charlotte calls them "peaceful tears." I am a blessed man. There is a great God who loves me, and He has prepared a place for me. Jesus calls that place, "My Father's House." There will be no tears there, probably because our heads won't be as big. I'm just saying, "Sometimes a cowboy rides away, sometimes he rides back home to stay." I'm thinking there will be butter beans and cornbread in heaven.

Chapter 16

Cubbie and Habakkuk

Our dog is depressed. I've mentioned our 13-year-old Corgi before, noting that he is quickly losing his eyesight. Because he can't see, he is easily startled, and at almost any sound will raise his head, perk up his ears, and look at us with his panic stare. He literally stays right under our feet, and we must always be on the alert to keep from tripping.

His official name is, CW's Dawson Cubbie. "CW" is a reference to Charlotte's college name, "Dawson" references our favorite Chicago Cub, Andre Dawson, and "Cubbie" because of our loyalty to the Cubs. CW's Dawson Cubbie is undoubtedly one of the best investments we've ever made. He is a good dog. These days, it is painful to watch him lying on the driveway watching over us and his domain, and yet unable to see anything beyond about 15 feet. We can see the uncertainty and confusion in his eyes.

We humans are also susceptible to depression, and for some of the same reasons as our dog. We can't see 15 feet into the future and most of us have never lived in such times of uncertainty. The sights, sounds, and possibilities startle us, and let's admit that we all have our panic stares. Adding to our fears are the uncertainties of a pandemic and the embarrassment of elected officials, and fellow citizens behaving like undisciplined 'yard dogs' and willing to do almost anything to be the Big Dog. It is depressing to see such disunity in the pack.

Yesterday, I was reading the Old Testament book of Habakkuk. In those 3 chapters the prophet is extremely honest with God concerning the cultural conditions surrounding him. Habakkuk looked at the world and was perplexed and fearful. He saw "violence" (1:2), "injustice" (v.3a), "destruction" (v.3c), "strife" and "conflict" (v.3d). Yet the Lord did not seem, to him, to be doing anything about it (vv.2–4). He saw pain and suffering and asked, *"How long, O Lord …? Why …?"* (vv.2–3). Habakkuk didn't seem to get a direct answer. However, he took his puzzled complaints and problems to God and left them with Him as he waited (2:1). God told him that he might have to wait for the answer: "Wait for it; it will certainly come and not delay" (v.3). While you wait for answers you are called to trust in God, even when you don't fully understand what He is doing. Habakkuk resolved to stay close to God whatever happened. He says, *"I will rejoice in the Lord, I will be joyful in God my Saviour. The Sovereign Lord is my strength; He makes my feet like the feet of a deer; He enables me to go on the heights."* (3:18-19) NASB)

I don't think our smart dog, Cubbie, has ever read the book of Habakkuk, but his response to his present dilemma is incredibly Biblical. I'm sure that he does not understand exactly what is happening. His uncertainty is obvious. He cannot see very far away. He is discouraged, even depressed. However, he is trusting in us more than ever. He is staying close to us. He is walking more by faith than by sight. He seems to know that we would never forsake him. He "sees" us as his provider, protector, and guide. He sleeps peacefully. I'm just saying that our dog, Cubbie, seems to be able to trust us more than most humans seem to be able to trust God. Good dog! Stay close.

Chapter 17

Freddie Lile Easterling

On October 6th, a dear friend and classmate lost his battle with leukemia and departed this life. I wanted to write something about our relationship in a way that I thought would be pleasing to him. Please pray for his wife of 48 years, Julie, his three children, and eight grandchildren. Freddie Lile Easterling (September 6, 1948–October 6, 2020)

Freddie and I have a lot of history. We have an incredible *Family History*. We share the same great grandparents: L.J. and Betty Bennett Purtle. Grandma Purtle was born in 1863 and lived to be 98 years old. She died in 1961; Freddie and I were 12 years old. We were two of her 111 (one hundred and eleven) great grandchildren. My first memory of Freddie was at one of Grandma Purtle's birthday celebrations; we were probably six or seven years old. A dozen or so of us boys, all cousins, slipped off after the potluck meal to the small pond at the backside of her property. We took off all our clothes and were swimming in that pond when one of our uncles showed up with a switch (that's a noun) and began to switch (that's a verb) every behind he could reach. I learned that day that Freddie and I were the fastest cousins at the party. Our mothers were first cousins, and they were very much alike; both were committed to Christ, family, and hard work. Freddie and I have a rich family history.

We also have an incredible *Friendship History*. We played on the same Little League baseball team; Freddie was a center fielder with a good arm, and I was a pitcher with a not-so-good arm. We both played on the all-star team, and I was on the mound when I delivered one of my not-so-fast fastballs. The batter hit it to dead center field, and it was headed out of the park when Freddie leaned over the fence and made the catch. I was so relieved that I walked all the way to center field just to shake his hand. It embarrassed him to death, and he said in his out of the side-of-his-mouth voice, "What in the world are you doing?"

One night, he was spending the night at our house after a baseball game, and we decided to sleep outside on quilts under the big shade tree. Sometime after midnight, we walked about a half mile up the highway and tied a string across the road. We hid in the ditch in some tall grass and waited for a car to drive by. I don't think either of us had any idea what was about to happen. A car came speeding down the highway, and when the car lights reflected off that string, the driver slammed on his brakes, almost running off the road. Three young men in their late teens or early twenties jumped out of the car and one of them ran right toward us yelling, "Here they are!" The two fast cousins jumped up and took off running as if there was an uncle with a switch right on our tails. We had not discussed an escape plan, so Freddie took off through the woods, and I, being more familiar with the terrain, took off up the clear-cut pipeline to a cut-through road. We both made it back to the quilt under the shade tree about the same time, but Freddie looked like he had run through a briar patch, which he pretty much had done.

Our friendship continued through junior high and high school as we continued to participate in sports together, especially football. We were part of the "19 Who Stayed" championship team of 1964, we were co-captains of the 1966 Bobcat team, and we both went to Henderson State University to compete for the few remaining scholarships along with 130 other hopeful athletes. Thanks to social media, and Facebook's

135

Famous Freddie's Friends, Fans, and Followers, we have remained close, and have expressed our love for each other many times. We have a rich Friendship History.

Thanks to our families, we also share an incredible *Faith History*, which goes back many generations. Our great grandparents were two of the seven charter members of a Baptist church established in 1886. That church is still alive, and seven generations of our family have attended there. We both grew up in church-going families and our parents were the real deal … genuine Christ-followers who loved God's Word and lived according to its teachings. During one of the most difficult and traumatic times of our high school lives, our fathers gathered around us in our living room and prayed for God's leadership and God's presence in our lives. Freddie and I were both given godly examples of a living faith. Freddie, like his parents, was committed to God, his family, and hard work. The older he grew, the more important his faith grew. In these last months, his faith has not disappointed as he has called upon the Lord for peace, and as we have all prayed for his peaceful transition into eternity.

A few weeks ago, we talked by phone, and he asked if I would speak at his funeral. There was a pause … I could not control my tears, and my voice cracked as I told him that it would be an honor. In typical Freddie fashion he said, "Cuz, you're crying more than I did when I got the news!" We have a rich Faith History.

We will also have an incredible *Future* together. We will be together in heaven for all of eternity because of our relationship with Jesus Christ. We both believe in the truth of Scripture, Jesus said to her, *"I am the resurrection and the life; he who believes in Me will live even if he dies, and everyone who lives and believes in Me will never die. Do you believe this?"* (John 11:25-26 NASB)

At a track meet in the Spring of 1967, our 880 relay team decided that we had run enough for the day. So, we talked Freddie into purposely getting two false starts (jump the gun), thereby disqualifying us from the race. We agreed to pay him $5 if he would do it. He did it, but in the most unconvincing way imaginable. He threw the baton down in disgust, as if he were so disappointed in himself for getting us disqualified. The Coach saw through what we were doing and made us run the race anyway.

Freddie has run the race and finished the course. As it turns out, he was the faster cousin because he has already made it home! My cousin beat us to the finish line, and he has passed on the baton of his legacy to his family, friends, fans, and followers. He will always be remembered as a good man with a good family, a good group of friends, a great faith, and now he is experiencing a rich future.

I'm just saying that I, for one, want to take up that baton and run with it. We will see you soon, Cuz.

Chapter 18

My Perspective-Adjuster

Perspective—*"the capacity to view things in their true relations or relative importance."* (Miriam Webster dictionary)

It is always helpful to view circumstances in their "relative importance." I have discovered a foolproof method of beginning each day with an adjusted perspective. Some of you are probably way ahead of me with this important solution to our tendency to focus way too much on our own misfortunes. Someone once shared with me that their perspective adjuster was, "There is always someone who would be willing to trade places with you." Whatever effective method you have found to move you from an attitude of gloom and doom to an attitude of contentment and thankfulness is important for your physical and spiritual health. If it works for you, please continue to utilize it consistently because a content and peaceful life really is a matter of perspective. But, if you are struggling with the negativity and uncertainty of living life in what appears to be an out-of-control culture, or if you are going through one of those "I don't think I can take much more" experiences, allow me to share my "perspective-adjuster" method.

I begin each morning by reading prayer requests from persecuted Christians. These are human beings who are being persecuted, ostracized, tortured, raped, and even killed, simply because they have chosen to believe that Jesus is the Son of God. Children who are not allowed to attend school, fathers who are fired from jobs, and families whose crops are burned and who are evicted from their villages because they will not renounce their faith in Jesus.

Recently I read of one communist government that was offering a bounty for information of any Christian gatherings. That is one reason why Christians all over the world have chosen to meet secretly and "whisper sing" their praises to the Lord. One Christian family in another communist nation could not sleep at night because their fellow villagers were constantly throwing cow dung through the windows of their house. They were told by authorities, "Your family will never be safe and have peace here in this village unless you stop believing in your God."

So, I begin each day with up-to-date reminders that, because of God's grace, I live in a country where I can *still* worship, sing, pray, read, and proclaim God's Word for as long and as loud as I desire. At the same time, I am given the great honor to pray for brothers and sisters in Christ whose commitment to our Savior is both a rebuke and a challenge to my own unchallenged, untested faith. Regardless of what I may be encountering in life, a good way to adjust my perspective is to start the day in humble gratefulness and intercessory prayer for those who will one day be seated on the front rows of heaven.

Several years ago, I had the privilege of visiting the burial site of Polycarp, the bishop of the church in Smyrna, who was martyred in A.D. 155. He was arrested and given the choice of cursing the name of Christ and making sacrifice to Caesar or death. One of the arresting officers pleaded with him, "What harm is it to say, 'Caesar is Lord' and to offer sacrifice and to be saved?" Polycarp's response as they prepared to burn him at the stake was, "Eighty and six years have I served Him, and He has done me no wrong. How can I blaspheme my King who saved me?"

I'm just saying that it's always good to view the "relative importance" of my problems.

Chapter 19

A Godly Mother

My mother was born on October 27, 1915. If she were still on earth, she would have just celebrated her 105th birthday. On the 27th, I sent a brief text to our children and older grandchildren to acknowledge her birthday and to remind them of a few of her qualities. I mentioned that she was, perhaps, the hardest working, and most selfless woman I had ever known.

As that day continued, I found myself thinking back to some of my earliest childhood memories. Before I was old enough to begin school, I stayed at home with my dad as he farmed while Mother went to her job at a local sewing company. I have vivid memories of a morning ritual before she would leave for work. She would sit in her 1940s platform rocking chair, and I would crawl up into her lap and say, "Bubber, rock me bye-bye one more time." Laugh all you want to, but I would not trade that memory for anything, and I was really upset when I was corrected and told that "Bubber" was supposed to be pronounced "Mother." It's just not the same!

I remember that she would always carry a fruit jar in her purse when we went to church on Sundays. She would fill the jar with ice cubes and water, wrap it tightly with "tin foil," and offer me a drink of cold water at exactly the right time during the preacher's sermon. Best drink of water ever. I never even had to tell her that I was thirsty.

Mother's go-to cure for all bumps, bruises, and nasty coughs was coal oil. A tablespoon of coal oil with a little bit of honey was her cure for the croup. I don't know if it really worked or if the taste was so bad, I just refused to cough again. She also kept a large bottle of "white liniment" for sore muscles. Its main ingredient was … you guessed it … coal oil. She had large, strong hands and she would rub out the soreness with that strong smelling liniment.

She was a country girl, known by all for her country cooking. She was a master in the kitchen, and she could put mountains of home-cooked food on the table in record time. Her annual two-week vacation was always taken when it was time to "put up" the beans, peas, corn, and squash from Dad's garden. Today, we would call that "a working vacation."

Mother departed this life for her eternal home in 1984 at the age of 68. Our five grandchildren never knew her, and most of my memories and stories about her are taken out of a time, context, and culture they do not understand. Words like 'No. 3 washtub', 'privy', 'dog trot porch', 'stove pipe', 'dairy barn', and 'milk can' are from a past that I hope are never a part of their future, but those words will always be a reminder that good memories are shaped by good people, and not necessarily by good circumstances.

Both of my parents were strong disciplinarians, but Dad was more New Testament while Mother was unashamedly Old Testament. She was a physically strong woman, and she did not mind using that strength to hold on to me with one hand and apply a belt to my backside with the other. I was 14 years old when, for the last time, she took me in our small bathroom for a well-deserved "whipping." In my mind, I was too old for my mother to whip me, so I managed to take the belt away from her. She sat down on the side of the bathtub and began to cry. No boy likes to make his mother cry, so I walked over to her, apologized, and gave her the belt. I voluntarily bent over the sink, all the time hoping that she would see the genuine remorse in my face. What was I thinking? I had it coming, and she delivered, but not with her usual full swing.

I disappointed her several times during my high school days, and it still hurts to know that I hurt her. But it seems that I made up for all the disappointments when, in 1968, I brought Charlotte Elizabeth Wilson home from college to introduce her to my parents. My wise mother immediately took a liking to Charlotte, and would grow to love her as much, if not more, than she loved me.

Today, October 29, 2020, Charlotte and I have been married 51 years. I have often said that without Charlotte, there would be no me. I would not, could not, be who I am today without my godly wife and those who know us best, know that is a true statement. Abraham Lincoln said, "No man is poor who has a godly mother." Proverbs 31:10 states, "An excellent wife, who can find? For her worth is far above jewels."

I'm just saying that I am one blessed man! Hallelujah!!

Chapter 20

Best Thanksgiving Ever

It was Thanksgiving morning 1985 and we awoke to the hardest rain we had ever experienced since living in Venezuela. Actually, it very rarely rained in our part of the country, and no one expected or prepared for this kind of downpour. Ours was the last house on a dead-end street, and the only drain for our street was right in front of our house. By mid-morning, it became obvious that the seldom-used drain was completely stopped up and the water level in front of our house was rising rapidly. I quickly grabbed the car keys to attempt to get our Ford Granada (assembled in Venezuela) off our street and safely parked on higher ground. There was already water in the car, but I was able to back it out to the main road. We realized that the only hope we had of keeping our house from being flooded was to unstop that non-functioning drain.

I need to explain that we loved living at the end of that dead end street. It was a pretty street in a nice neighborhood, and located just a few blocks from Lake Maracaibo, the largest lake in South America. On this particular Thanksgiving Day, it seemed that most of the rainwater on our side of the city was trying to make its way to that lake, and our street was the route of choice. Thus, the importance of the infamous drain located just in front of our house.

The ground in our city had no idea what to do with this much water, being accustomed to 15-minute showers a half dozen times a year. The hard packed dirt simply rejected the deluge and funneled it down our street. We placed towels on the floor at every door. We move the furniture upstairs, leaving only the piano and the hutch in the downstairs living room. The rain continued and we were losing the battle. I looked at Kyle, who was 15 at the time, and said, "We've got to unstop that drain." We waded into the waist deep water and as I, using my long arms, began reaching down into the drain, it became apparent that we were not alone in the water. Rats, large rats, began to circle us like sharks around chum. We deducted that they were tiring from treading water, and viewed us as possible life rafts. Kyle, with his trusty broom handle, began using his "Whack-a-Mole" skills to keep the rats away, but it was even scarier when they would disappear out of sight under the water. To this day I will run from a rat of any size.

Meanwhile, Charlotte was in the kitchen, standing in ankle-deep water determined to prepare a Thanksgiving feast for our family and our friends from Caracas who were trapped in a nearby hotel. Kenneth, who was six, was running barefoot through the water yelling, "This is the best Thanksgiving ever!" At this point, the rain is still pouring down, and Charlotte has had enough. She says, "We need to pray!" So, we stood outside in the pouring rain and asked God for a miracle. Within minutes, the rain stopped, the cursed drain began flowing freely, and the water level began to rapidly recede. By mid-afternoon, we sat down in our dry house with our friends and celebrated a most memorable Thanksgiving Day.

The year 2020 could also provide a very interesting Thanksgiving Day. Some states are implementing some new regulations for Thanksgiving celebrations, and I will leave it up to you to determine if these are necessary, ridiculous, or somewhere in between. Probably your celebration may look different and feel different this year … it's just been that kind of year. I'm just saying that even if you are standing in waist-deep water fighting off rats the size of large cats, you can still have "the best Thanksgiving ever!" Surely, we can all find things for which we are thankful … like broom handles.

Chapter 21

Hallmark Movies

Dear Hallmark, I am a faithful fan of your movies. I have watched so many of your movies that I know exactly when the important scenes are going to occur. My two favorite scenes are the "almost kiss," and the big "final kiss," which normally happens under mistletoe or when it starts snowing. My least favorite scene is the "misunderstanding" or "false assumption."

As a retired pastor watching these false assumptions play out, I sometimes want to scream at the screen, "Communication! Communication! Communication!" Just one time I would like to see him/her just tell the truth at the right moment. Don't sit on the truth until the jealous loser guy or the vengeful ex-girlfriend comes racing into the barn dance and reveals that you initially came into town to turn Happyville into a theme park!

I do, however, like the way your characters always clear up those misunderstandings, and loser guy and vengeful girl are always so understanding and cooperative at the breakup. If they had always been that attentive and understanding back in the big city, there might have been more hope for them. The small-town environment seems to revive their relationship skills. Maybe just once, loser guy and vengeful girl could stay in Happyville, get married and run the bookstore/bakery/tree farm. They might not deserve a snowfall kiss scene, but maybe they could lead the countdown at Happyville's Christmas tree lighting ceremony.

Initially, I did not notice the mishaps in some of your movies, but my wife caught them immediately. Things like plastic flowers planted in a flower bed, green oak trees in the background during a "snowfall," falling snow that never gets stuck in the blond girl's hair, and guitar players who never change chords can't get by her creative eye. By the way, do those pianos even work?

I am not writing to be critical because, as I said, I am a real fan. I will even watch those "Royal" shows about a king, prince, or royal whatever that take place in an unknown 'Vania, 'Lovia, 'Vokia, or 'Astan. Those are my least favorites, but probably because I never learned to dance with my chin held so high.

The purpose of my letter is purely selfish. I would like to appear in one of your movies. I'm not asking for a speaking role, just an appearance. Maybe I could be the guy at the hot chocolate stand, or one of the shoppers at the craft show, or just standing in the crowd at that Christmas tree lighting. I was watching one of your movies today and I noticed the same lady at the cookie contest, in the crowd at the Christmas show, and backstage after the show. She had three appearances in one movie, and she never said a word or smiled. At least I can smile. I would not require a wardrobe because I have a scarf. I would be willing to drive to Alberta or Vancouver, or wherever you're filming next spring. It means that much to me. Appearing in a Hallmark movie is on my bucket list and that bucket is closer to my foot than it's ever been.

Thank you so much for your movies and keep up the good work. I have noticed in the past eight months that a lot of residents in large cities are moving to smaller communities. I'm sure it's because of your movies and the way small towns encourage healthy relationships.

Oh, Happy Thanksgiving. Obviously, you don't celebrate that holiday … just saying.

147

Chapter 22

A Christmas Poem

Please remember that this is my first attempt, that it is not my lane, and that I was a physical education major. Just saying …

She Gave Birth

Such a humble birth.
There has never been a humbler one on earth.
There were no witnesses there. She gave birth,
a virgin girl with no one to provide her care.

And what of Joseph, a faithful man with questions,
whose answers he could not humanly understand.
Two more insignificant characters the world has never
known,
yet chosen by their sovereign God to nurture and care
for His very own.

Majesty born near a cattle stall, majesty coming into
this earth,
yet purposely hidden from all.
Born in such a way so He could relate to all mankind.
Born of the Spirit, so in Him alone salvation they could find.

It is a perfect story born in the perfect mind of God.

Written by the Spirit and recorded by faithful men with
whom this Savior would trod.

He would live a perfect life in a sinful, godless world.

He would die a cruel death, on a cross, as He looked down
into the face of that Jewish virgin girl.

"She gave birth," and now, she was standing there,

as He gave His life to redeem and save this one so fair.

How beautiful the perfect story of this faithful Jewish girl,

who said "Yes" to God in a less-than-perfect world.

As the Holy One hung there upon the cross, fulfilling
His divine Father's will,

His human heart was focused on His loving mother, still.

"Woman, behold thy son …" as He placed her in the
Beloved's care.

As He is dying on that cross, the Holy One remembers,
"she gave birth" when no one else was there.

It's a perfect story born in the perfect mind of God.

"When the fullness of time had come" … a perfect birth,
a perfect life upon this earth did trod.

He came for the perfect reason, to pay for our sin on earth.

It's no wonder that we worship when we read that she
gave birth.

*"And she gave birth to her firstborn son; and she wrapped Him
in cloths, and laid Him in a manger, because there was no room for
them in the inn."* (Luke 2:7 NASB)

*"When Jesus then saw His mother, and the disciple whom He
loved standing nearby, He *said to His mother, "Woman, behold,*

your son!" Then He *said to the disciple, "Behold, your mother!" From that hour the disciple took her into his own household." (John 19:26-27 NASB)

"But when the fullness of the time came, God sent forth His Son, born of a woman, born under the Law, so that He might redeem those who were under the Law, that we might receive the adoption as sons." (Galatians 4:4-5 NASB)

Chapter 23

Just Passing Through

(I wrote this about two months ago, but never felt at peace about posting it until now. Like you, I'm just trying to deal with my own emotions, not suggesting I have an opinion that covers all bases.)

This world is not my home,
I'm just a passing through.
My treasures are laid up
Somewhere beyond the blue.
The angels beckon me from heaven's open door,
And I can't feel at home in this world anymore.

If you were singing those words instead of reading them, you are really old, and/or you probably listened to Southern gospel music as a child. That old song, "This World Is Not My Home," was written in 1936. I woke up a few weeks ago singing those words in my mind, and now, not only can I not stop singing them, but they have also become my go-to response as I see and hear things in today's world.

This world was never meant to be our final home. From the moment of conception, we begin a short, brief journey as visitors to a foreign land. As we "are just a passing through" this world, we are preparing our lives, and the lives of as many others as possible, for an eternal existence in a very real eternal home. Our eternal address depends not so much on what kind of life we live as we "pass through," but rather on how we respond to the One who lived a perfect life. Jesus, who lived that perfect life, warned us all about getting too attached to this world and the things of this world. He wanted us to be so free from the influences of this world that we could honestly say, "my treasures are laid up somewhere beyond ..." Nothing should ever distract us from that eternal focus.

Personally, I don't like the direction this world seems to be headed. I am able to identify with less and less of current "thinking." I feel a restlessness that I've never felt before. No angels are speaking to me "from heaven's open door," but I sure think about my eternal home a lot more than I ever have.

The only voice I'm hearing seems to be saying, "You are not of this world, but I have chosen for you to be in it until I choose to call you home." So, as I watch a world going crazier, I must remind myself that all of this is temporary, and that God thoroughly and completely loves all the world, not the worldliness, but the world—all of us. I find myself repeatedly saying in my mind, "God loves him. Christ died for her. How can God love me?"

My instructions have been spelled out for me in *The Guidebook for Living Temporarily In A Foreign Land.* I'm sure you also received a copy. The instruction that seems to best apply to this brief span of history is found on page 1035 of my Guidebook: ... *"but sanctify Christ as Lord in your hearts, always being ready to make a defense to everyone who asks you to give an account for the hope that is in you, yet with gentleness and reverence ..."* (1 Peter 3:15 NASB).

There are many other important instructions, but this one seems to have my name on it.

What is occurring before our eyes is a very real spiritual struggle, not for who runs our nation, but who rules our hearts.

I may not "feel at home in this world anymore," but while I'm still in this world, I cannot ignore the eternal consequences of this struggle. People who do not have the hope of heaven are going to live, think, and act as if life in this world is everything. Not only is it not everything, but it is also not anything, compared to our eternal existence.

I'm just saying that while we're waiting for the angels to "beckon us from heaven's open door," we have a significant assignment to "give an account for the hope that is in us."

That old song says, "O, Lord, you know I have no friend like you; If heaven's not my home, then Lord what would I do?"

A good question that needs to be considered by us all.

Chapter 24

Snowed In

Ten inches may not be a lot of snow, unless you live in South Arkansas, or unless you are a Corgi dog who is only 12 inches tall. In addition, our 13-year-old Corgi, Cubbie, is blind in one eye and has very limited vision in his good eye. We refuse to say that he is blind. Also, I need to mention that he cannot hear and gets easily confused when he cannot follow one of his familiar and well-used trails.

He and I are on the same night-time bathroom schedules, so when I took him out at 3 a.m. Monday morning, the snow was not yet that deep and he made it to his favorite winter-time morning spot (the one closest to the house) without any difficulty. By mid-afternoon, it was like Cubbie had been "walled-in" by snow piles up to his eyes. It was painful to watch as he would take off in the direction of one of his bathroom spots only to walk directly into a snow wall. You could almost see in his expression, "Who put this wall here. It wasn't here yesterday. How am I gonna get to my spot?" He would not make use of any of our emergency potty creations, not even the plywood-covered "walkthrough" that Charlotte designed using large flowerpots.

So, with shovel and broom in hand, we cleared a 20-yard path through the back yard to the edge of the woods … his favorite afternoon spot. I won't tell you how long it took us, but we finally reached the sacred grounds and brought Cubbie outside on his leash. We waited patiently as he sniffed, and sniffed, and sniffed, and then turned and headed back to the house. Failure.

For the next few hours, we tried to coax our confused dog to do his business in several new potty spots, but he wasn't having it. Finally, around 5:30 on Monday afternoon, I opened the back door and guided Cubbie down the 20-yard cleared pathway in the back yard. He walked all the way down the path until his nose bumped against the snow wall, made a 180-degree turn and made his contribution to the 2021 Snow "Apoopalypse." He trotted back up the pathway like the weight of the world had been lifted … or dumped.

Tomorrow is a new day. The Weather Channel is predicting another 10 inches of snowfall. I'm just saying that Cubbie and I are ready for the "dog days of summer."

Chapter 25

Letters from Home

For the past several days, Charlotte and I have been totally immersed in dozens and dozens of war-time letters written by her father from 1943–1946. These letters just came into our possession this week.

He and his parents exchanged almost weekly letters sent from Dumas, Arkansas, and several remote locations in the Southwest Pacific. Her dad was 19 years old, but near the end of the war, at age 21, he wrote more than once about how old he felt. His last assignment was in occupied Japan after the bombing of Hiroshima, and he describes himself as "one of the old men who has not yet shipped home." His letters, like other letters from "our boys," were full of thoughts about home and home cooking, but noticeably void of details about exactly where he was and what he was facing. Knowing the infantry unit to which he was attached, seventy-five years later, we were able to read about their battles and follow his footsteps through New Guinea and the Philippine jungles. He was a superior marksman assigned to a machine gun squad. That told us a lot.

His letters, especially those written to his father, almost always touched on squirrel or quail seasons. You could sense in his words that he was vicariously walking behind those dogs, Bonnie, and Mac, as they hunted the familiar woods and fields back home. Even his mother would write that "dad has killed a mess of birds," and aunt or uncle so-and-so were "coming over for supper."

He wrote about his "buddies" and it seems that they were not only good soldiers, but also good chicken catchers. A fried chicken dinner (the Southern boys always made gravy) seemed to be as uplifting as a letter from home, although the latter met and satisfied a different kind of longing. His letters would almost always mention how many letters he had received and how much he appreciated not only the letters, but also the cookies, cakes, tee shirts, and most importantly, family pictures.

His mother's letters were the most touching of all. She had three sons serving in the Army and her life revolved around keeping in touch with all of them. It was difficult for the brothers to keep up with each other, so Mom became the messenger. I'm sure she would write the same message to all three, but she would always end Charlotte's dad's letters with "be a good boy." Only a mom would say that to a 19-year-old soldier fighting for his life in a dense jungle thousands of miles from home. It was as if she would not dare go where she needed to with all the emotions about to burst forth as she thought about her sons, and the only way she could express it was, "Be a good boy." Can't you feel those words?

I never met Charlotte's dad. He did not adjust well after his return home in 1946. As someone has said, "Some came back with wounds that don't bleed …" and that is a very accurate description of the father-in-law I never met.

However, you cannot read about World War II (or any war) and not be humbled by the sacrifice and bravery of our soldiers and their families. Most of us have no idea, not a clue, what it's like to be waiting day after day for a letter from home.

I'm just saying, thank you sir (and all others) for your service and sacrifice.

Chapter 26

Ordering at a Drive-Thru

I hate ordering food in a Drive-Thru...any kind of food at any place in the world that sells food. Before I even approach the garbled speaker system to attempt to place an order, I am gripping the steering wheel in total intimidation and dread. From three cars back, I am straining to read the Menu sign just to practice my order, all the time hearing my inner voice saying, "You will not get it right, not today, not tomorrow, not ever."

It is very difficult for me to understand the sounds coming from the menu sign. Okay, my hearing is not what it used to be, but I can still hear static. I never understand the speaker's first words, but I just assume it is asking me for my order. I still feel weird about yelling at a sign, but I learned a long time ago that you must hang your head and left shoulder out of the car window to communicate to a sign.

The real fun begins after I have given my order to the sign. The following is exactly what happened to me less than one hour ago:

Sign: "Orhissss bzzzzz hissss."

Me: "Yes, I would like the No. 1 chicken tenders spicy, fries, and a large, sweet tea, no ice please."

Sign: "Do you want those tenders mild or spicy?"

Me: "Spicy."

Sign: "What side would you like?"

Me: "Fries."

Sign: "Would you like a biscuit or a roll?"

Me: "Neither."

Sign: "And what would you like to drink?"

Me: "Large, sweet tea, no ice please."

Sign: "Did you say, 'No ice?'"

Me: "Yes."

Sign: (Long pause) "Do you mean, 'Yes, no ice or yes, you want ice?'"

Me: "No ice."

Sign: "Okay, that will be "Hiss…bzzzz."

By that time, I wasn't even hungry. Obviously, I don't speak "menu" because somewhere between placing the order, paying for the food I just ordered, and receiving my paid-for food order, something always goes wrong.

So, I arrive home with the order (which was for my 14-year-old granddaughter), she opens the sack and says disappointedly, "You didn't get fries?"

Me: "Well, at least there's no ice in your Dr Pepper."

I'm just saying, hisssss…bbzzzz.

Chapter 27

Sunday Worship

This past Sunday was my first time to physically be in church since March 2020. It was a little strange seeing marked-off pews, masked worshippers, and fist bumps instead of handshakes and hugs, but, for me, being there in person sure beats online worship.

I watched a dad, mom, and three children walk in together and take their seats a few pews in front of us. I had one of those flashback moments to 40 years ago when Charlotte and I were a young couple with three children. At age 32, we were living in Oklahoma City, and I was pastoring a great church. They were a praying church and I know they were praying for this young pastor and his family. I had only been out of seminary for four years and was unqualified to lead a church of this size, but they prayed, and God blessed.

Unknown to me, there were three faithful ladies in that church who had been praying for years that God would call missionaries from their church family. Sure enough, their prayers were answered, and God called Charlotte and me to serve as missionaries in Venezuela. Every one of those sweet memories passed through my mind in "a split second," as I watched that young family settle into their seats and prepare for worship.

Since returning to the States from Venezuela in 1989, I very rarely attend a church service without thinking of our Venezuelan worship experiences—simple, genuine, heartfelt, happy, refreshing worship, and most of the time, full of surprises.

At first, those surprises bothered us simply because we were not yet familiar with Venezuelan culture.

During one of my first preaching experiences at a small Venezuelan Baptist church, an elderly lady on one side of the church stood up and began carrying on a conversation with a lady on the other side of the church. I had no idea what was going on, but I noticed that no one else was bothered, so I kept on stumbling through one of my first Spanish sermons. After the service, a missionary colleague told me the lady was telling her friend that family was coming for lunch, and she had to catch the bus and get home.

I will never forget the vicious dogfight in the back of one church as I was preaching and the comment of our friend, Evaluz. She seemed unmoved by the commotion, took a quick glance at the two dogs, and said, "They both need to be in church."

I was preaching in a downtown church where windows and doors were always left open for the benefit of passersby on the busy street. It was not unusual for people to just stroll in or hang over a window ledge out of interest or curiosity. I was preaching out of the New Testament and kept repeating the Spanish phrase, "Jesus dijo," (Jesus said). One of the curious onlookers, who may have been out a little late the night before, stepped into the aisle and yelled, "That's a lie! My name is Jesus, and I didn't say any of that!" He was politely escorted outside, and the sermon continued.

Well, back to this past Sunday. It was great seeing my church family, hearing the live music, and being present to hear our pastor's message. At the end of the service, our pastor introduced two new members and one of those was a college student from Colombia. I could not wait to greet her and hear her speak the "heavenly language." She seemed just as pleased to meet me as we talked about Venezuelan arepas and Colombian coffee. It was an unexpected and pleasant surprise.

I'm just saying, if you've not made it back to church since Covid, go this Sunday. You might be in for a pleasant surprise.

Chapter 28

Time Is Not on Our Side

I won't bore you with all the details, but I have seen more doctors, had more tests, and showed my Medicare card more in the last nine months than I could have ever imagined. Nothing severe, just some of those things that come with lots of mileage.

It started with a few late-night visits to our local ER with no real answers, but a later appointment with a gastroenterologist revealed a H. Pylori bacteria in my stomach. After three weeks of antibiotics and not a lot of relief, the gallbladder became the suspect, but something called the PIPIDA scan was inconclusive. Having gallbladder problems is something like not being able to prove guilt because all you have is circumstantial evidence. No surgeon will touch it without absolute proof of guilt. Finally, an MRI on Christmas Eve provided the needed proof … gallbladder was the culprit and surgery was the long-awaited answer.

But wait, I failed to mention the allergic reaction to a prescribed medication that resulted in a near hospitalization. My entire body was covered with a red rash, and I peeled two different layers of skin. One month of steroids and a compromised immune system delayed the gallbladder surgery until this past week. I am now recovering and thankful. I am not asking for sympathy. We all know that the medical conditions I have experienced are minor compared to what some of you and some of our friends and families have gone and are going through. What really got my attention these past nine months was not my struggle with health issues, but my continuing struggle with Time. It never stops … Time, that is. Time doesn't seem to care a great deal about what's going on in our lives; it just keeps insensitively ticking. Life itself is characterized by the ticking of Time, but Time, it seems, doesn't care much about life. If Time cared, it would stop or at least slow down while we are dealing with great joy, great loss, or great pain.

I first noticed this insensitive, uncaring side of Time when my mother died in 1984. Our friends and family were gracious in their outpouring of love and support, but it upset me that Time did not stop to recognize my mother's greatness. Instead of pausing for just a second to honor her, Time just kept on ticking and the day was gone, and then a week, and then a month, and now it's 2021, and Time has never stopped. Time is like that.

During this past year, our grandchildren all had birthdays, our only grandson got married, our children have made important career decisions, my wife has nursed me through one medical issue after another, several of our friends have suffered the loss of loved ones, and Time seems insensitive to it all. Time gives no time to take the time to enjoy or mourn life-changing events.

My other dispute with Time is its ever-increasing velocity. Ok, so it can't stop or even slow down, but why does it have to speed up when we're going downhill?

How did it get so late so soon?
It's night before it's afternoon
December is here before it's June.
My goodness how the time has flown.
How did it get so late so soon?
(attributed to Dr. Seuss)

Time does march on and what your parents told you is true, the longer you live, the faster Time flies. It's one of those illogical facts. I am very familiar with the passage in Ecclesiastes 3:1, *"There is an appointed time for everything. And there is a time for every event under heaven-..."* (NASB). I have no problem with the *"a times."* I understand that we will all celebrate and mourn various life events. I am not questioning the sovereignty of God, nor am I blaming God or struggling with a crisis of faith. I'm just saying that at times, I would like to slow down Time … just for a moment, to take it all in. A little more Time to laugh, to celebrate, to grieve properly, to heal inwardly, to contemplate seriously, to learn spiritually.

Time is not going to stop or recognize our plea for it to just slow down. Time does what God designed it to do. It marches. Knowing this, God says to us in a loving yet commanding way, *"Therefore, be careful how you walk, not as unwise men but as wise, making the most of your time, because the days are evil."* (Ephesians 5:15-16 NASB)

I'm just saying that Time may not be on our side, but God is.

Chapter 29

Spiritual Markers

I graduated from Henderson State University in May 1971, 50 years ago. That would make me a Golden Reddie, which really sounds confusing considering when you mix the colors gold and red you get sparkling red, which sounds like something I shouldn't know much about. By the way, for those of you still asking, "What is a Reddie?" check out #nomerebeast narrated by my long-time friend and teammate, Bobby Jones.

I arrived on the campus of HSU in August of 1967. I was there to pursue a BSE degree and to play football, not necessarily in that order. Upon arrival, I checked into the athletic dorm and my first memory is lying on my bed, looking out the second-floor window, and watching unknown teammates walk out the front door heading toward the cafeteria. Those guys looked huge! I didn't know any of them at the time, but the guys I saw were two offensive tackles, four defensive linemen, and a 6'7" tight end. They would soon become dear friends, but on that day, at first sight, they looked extremely intimidating. I was silently, but seriously questioning my ability to compete with guys that large at the college level. I remember being very afraid. However, I overcame that initial fear and played four years for the Reddies, and graduated with a BSE and a decent GPA. During that time, I also met and married Charlotte, and that was the greatest blessing of my Henderson days.

So, 50 years after my college graduation, our oldest grandchild will be graduating as a doctor of occupational therapy from the University of Central Arkansas. Alexa Nicole Corley has tackled more obstacles, worked harder, and certainly displayed more discipline than her Papa. Alexa told me, "It's a 'clinical doctorate,' so you wouldn't necessarily call me Doctor Corley …," but you can bet your sparkling red that she will be Doctor Corley to me. She, and our other four grandchildren, might very well be among our greatest contributions. There are few things as rewarding as watching grandchildren take faith steps, and make wise life choices.

Obviously, I had no way of looking into the future and predicting what life would be like as I walked downstairs and made my way to the cafeteria in 1967. In many ways, it was a step of faith despite internal fear, and there would be many of those faith steps in the next fifty-plus years. Without even realizing it, that walk to the cafeteria was a spiritual marker that would lead me to lifelong friendships, to my future wife, to a renewed faith, to a call of God upon our lives, to multiple opportunities to see the power of God at work in my own life and the lives of others.

For many reasons, that step of faith over fifty years ago has proven to be one of the wisest steps in my life.

Looking back and reflecting upon the spiritual markers in your life is a valuable exercise. It will remind you of the incredible, loving guidance of the omniscient hand of God. It will also reassure you that you can entrust your future generations to the same loving hands. Only God knew in 1967 that our first grandchild would become such a hard-working, disciplined student, and a daily Christ-follower. If I had known all of this fifty-four years ago, I would have run down those steps and sprinted to the cafeteria.

I'm just saying that taking steps of faith in the direction you believe to be the will of God can, in time, bring forth an abundant harvest. God works like that.

Chapter 30
Country Church Funerals

I just returned from a second cousin's funeral. I have a lot of cousins, but as I looked around the church crowd today, it hit me hard that I am from the oldest living branch of the family tree. In my mother's family, there were 15 first cousins and only 3 of us are still alive. I am the youngest at age 72. Now, in 2021, there are so many grandchildren and great grandchildren that it baffles the mind, and it is both humbling and alarming when one of the younger ones comes up and says, "I've heard my grandparents talk about you."

I trust you to understand when I say that I love country church funerals. If you were raised in a country church, you will probably understand why I say that. There is a sincerity, a simplicity, and a genuine heartfelt sympathy that seems to, at least temporarily, lessen the grief of losing a loved one.

Today, I was struck by the undivided attention given to the bi-vocational pastor as he humbly admitted that he was totally trusting in the Word of God to minister to all of us. He had known this family all his life, and they knew of his credibility. To me as a retired pastor, there is nothing sweeter than a community's trust in a God-called pastor.

I fought back tears as two of my cousins, sisters, sang an old song that was destined to be sung at country church funerals. *Beulah Land* always sounds better in a country church.

As the obituary was read and kind comments were being made about my cousin, I noticed a mom changing seats to sit next to, and put her arm around her son. I guessed him to be about 12 years old, and he was fighting back tears. I learned later that he was a neighbor's child and, obviously, felt very close to my cousin.

As I watched him struggle with his emotions, I traveled back in time to the first funeral I attended. I was seven years old, and it was the funeral for one of those 14 first cousins. I remembered putting my hands over my eyes, placing my head in my dad's lap, and crying uncontrollably. I kept my eye on that young man throughout the service and I could identify with his grief, and I could feel what he was feeling.

Another thing I enjoy about country church funerals is that a lot of times it is a short walk to the cemetery. Family, friends, neighbors, generations walking together to lay a loved one to rest. Even for a grieving family, it is a peaceful walk when you are doing it together. Country cemeteries have always seemed more peaceful to me.

Of course, after the service, there was plenty of food … country cooking. The small children, the ones on newer branches of the family tree, got out of those church clothes in record time and enjoyed being with their cousins. It brought back memories as I sat next to my 90-year-old cousin, and we talked about times when we were the new branches. He talked about my dad, and I talked about his, and we were the only two in the room that shared those particular memories. Before I left, I promised to visit him in the Nursing Home and at that moment I needed my mom to sit next to me and put her arm around me.

I'm just saying that there's nothing like a country church funeral to remind you of the importance of family trees and how quickly they grow.

Chapter 31

The Inner Desire to Write

Since I started this writing thing, I have discovered that, for me, the hardest thing about writing is getting started. There are moments when I feel the need to write, but I really don't have anything to write about. So, I decide to wait for an idea, a prompting, or an occurrence that gives me inspiration, but that inner desire just to write something remains and it will not go away until I put words on a page. I don't understand that about myself, and I don't know if that's normal or completely weird, but now you know why I write … I write because I need to.

My first attempt to satisfy that inner desire to write came in the eighth grade. At a junior high basketball tournament, my teammates and I met a group of cheerleaders from another town. We exchanged addresses and a few days later while sitting in Study Hall, I "needed" to write the dark-haired girl. Telling her that I was writing the letter during Study Hall didn't seem bold and daring enough, so I told her that I was writing the letter while "sitting in my very boring English class." I was very pleased with my first few paragraphs, and I put the unfinished letter in my notebook to wait for further inspiration.

I accidentally left the unfinished letter in my desk after my next class, which was … you guessed it … English. Realizing what I had done, I rushed back into the English classroom to retrieve the letter. Too late. My English teacher had found the letter, and not only was she reading it, but she was also correcting the grammar with her red pen.

I tried my best to explain that I did not write the letter while sitting in her classroom, but she just kept reading the phrase, "sitting in my very boring English class." She never believed me and later that day, I heard her telling the story to other teachers in the hallway. I never finished that letter, but I'm sure the dark-haired girl would have been touched by my attempt to impress her.

The "need" to write has increased immensely since I retired in 2016, but this time the motivation has been different, and more intense. Two years ago, I started writing stories about people in whom God's activity was obvious, and, in many cases, miraculous. While participating in over 50 mission trips, I kept bullet-point notes of events, people, and especially of Divine appointments. Some of those notes are 30+ years old, but as I re-read them I could see the faces, the places, and sense the same presence of God. It was amazing.

So, I've written a book! I "needed" to write it and it was published in 2021. When I needed someone to edit it, I first thought of my 8th grade English teacher, but she is no longer available. I contacted my longtime Henderson Reddie friend Dennis Byrd, who has years of newspaper editing experience, and he has walked me through the process and turned words on a page into a real book. I'm just saying that *Just Outside of Hope* by Stan Parris is something I needed to do.

Chapter 32

Different Life Callings

Yesterday, I had a one-and-a-half-hour phone conversation with my cousin-brother, Jim Hartsfield. Jim and his wife, Suzi, live in Arizona, where most of the population have upper leg scars from encountering scorching seat belts during the long, hot summers. Sure, it's a dry heat, but the seat belts don't know the difference. A metal seatbelt that has been simmering for hours in a 115-degree Arizona sun becomes an instrument of torture. Trust me.

Jim is a retired firefighter and during the phone call, I asked him some questions about his career. Honestly, these were questions I wish I had asked him years ago. I have always admired him for choosing to be a fireman/EMT, especially knowing first-hand of his tendency to faint at the sight of blood.

My greatest contribution to humanity may have been the summer afternoon when I pulled a drowning Jim out of Papa Parris' horse trough (actually it was a #3 wash tub). He accidentally cut his thumb and knelt at the water trough to wash it off. When he saw the blood streaming up through the water, he turned as pale as milk, and slumped headfirst into old Mollie's drinking water. He was almost all the way in when I grabbed his belt and pulled him out and gently laid him on the smelly dirt of the barnyard. Jim swears he does not remember this, but he was unconscious, and he would never admit that his six-year-old little cousin saved his life.

I remember how shocked we were to learn that college-age Jim was working for an independent ambulance service. They were taking calls outside the city limits of Yuma, Arizona, and some calls even took them near the Mexican border. They made the decision to add a fire service to their business when they learned of four Hispanic children dying in a house fire where no fire service existed. Fireman Jim has always had a tender heart.

They located a fire truck in Oklahoma and Jim and a co-worker flew to Tulsa, made the purchase, and drove the fire truck back to Arizona. Somewhere around Albuquerque, they came upon an 18-wheeler on fire. They pulled up behind the truck with their flashing lights, and then advised the driver that they had no water. In fact, they didn't even have a fire extinguisher. As they continued their trip, they were the first on the scene of a one-car accident near Gila Bend. They treated the female driver, and then at her request, placed her in the fire truck and gave her a ride to her home in Yuma.

Our phone conversation covered a lifetime, and he continued to talk both about the serious moments and the light-hearted moments. My admiration for my cousin-brother grew as he mentioned lives lost and lives saved during his career. He stays in touch with many of his brother firefighters, and among them there exists a well-deserved mutual respect.

I'm glad we had that phone call and I mentioned to Jim that he should consider writing about his career, but he mentioned that writing was not his calling. I hope we can have more of those conversations while we both can still remember, still communicate, and still hear each other.

I'm just saying that we can learn a lot by taking time to ask the right questions of a retiree. Then, as we take time to listen, we might discover some silent, humble heroes. I'm also just saying that different life callings require different hats; Jim was called to wear a fireman's hat.

Chapter 33

Peace

As a child, the barn on our home place was not only a place for cows, feed, and bales of hay, it was also a place of imagination, refuge, and solace. I spent hours in that barn playing, thinking, and feeling safe. Its high loft was my favorite spot, especially when it was full of hay bales. I can't remember all the games I invented playing in that loft while climbing on the bales and looking out through the large window-like opening, but I remember my favorite. Oh, I loved to take my BB gun, climb the ladder from inside one of the stalls, and spend a Saturday afternoon pretending to save the ranch, or protect the wagon train, and then to be seriously wounded, causing me to fall from the very top of the bales of hay, rolling and rolling to the loft floor. I was great at falling, but that was not my favorite game.

My favorite was not really a game, it was a place in that hayloft where I could go and literally feel peace. In that special place, peace was as real to me as hay in the barn. Every year when the hayloft was full to the top, I would burrow a tunnel through the bales all the way to the back wall of the barn. There I would create a kind of hidden fort, right in front of a small window that allowed me to look out over the barn lot, and more importantly, allowed me to breathe fresh air. I would spend hours hidden away in my secret place of refuge. I would not refer to it as my "happy place," and being an extremely loved only child, I didn't really need a "safe place," but I found it to be so peaceful.

Alone, but knowing that I was not alone—that kind of peace has such a presence.

I'm not a kid anymore, the barn is no longer there, and if I fell from the top of a haystack, I would be much more than seriously wounded. However, I still love to burrow through whatever obstacles or circumstances that are in the way of my getting to that peaceful place of refuge, solace, and secluded shelter. The older I get the more I desire not just to spend some time there, but to abide there, to dwell there ... where peace is a literal presence.

I'm pretty sure that the Psalmist, David, never played in a hay barn, but he sure knew about a place of refuge, solace, and shelter. His inspired words say it all: *"He who dwells in the shelter of the Most High will abide in the shadow of the Almighty. I will say to the Lord, "My refuge and my fortress, My God, in whom I trust!" For it is He who delivers you from the snare of the trapper And from the deadly pestilence. He will cover you with His pinions, And under His wings you may seek refuge; His faithfulness is a shield and bulwark."* (Psalms 91:1-4 NASB)

There have been times in my adult life when I have felt the need to crawl through the tunnel to the back wall of that old barn, to curl up in that tiny hideout, and just stay there until things were better. Then I remember that the peace, solace, and presence that I really need are not found under a haystack. Jesus said, *"Peace I leave with you; My peace I give to you; not as the world gives do I give to you. Do not let your heart be troubled, nor let it be fearful."* (John 14:27 NASB1995)

I'm just saying that the presence of Jesus can be your "happy place," your "safe place," and the place where peace is literally His presence. If you feel the need to crawl away to a secluded hideout, just try breathing deeply, and slowly saying my favorite word, "Peace." He'll hear and understand.

Chapter 34

How's the Weather

Much has been written about the differences between men and women, the differences in certain personality types, and the fact that some of us just look at things differently than others. For example, seated in our favorite chairs, sipping our first cup of morning coffee, I comment to Charlotte, "There's a 30 percent chance of rain this afternoon." My brainiac wife quickly responds, "Yea, and there is a storm on Jupiter the size of the earth."

Anyone who knows us can testify that Charlotte and I are very different. Those differences are no more obvious than when it comes to how we follow the weather. My weather app tells me very little more than what I can determine by walking outside. Her weather app apparently can show tornadoes that might be developing in Sri Lanka. She occasionally will show me on her app how many lightning strikes are occurring within fifty miles. My response, "I don't care if it's lightning in Horatio, I'm looking out the window and it ain't lightning in the front yard."

My weather attitude goes all the way back to my 1950s childhood when the radio announcer would warn of a tornado having been spotted in our area. Immediately, all the men would go outside and look into the pitch-black sky, looking and listening for real proof of a tornado. Even though today we have the capabilities to track a storm, and predict its location and arrival, I still have this internal pull to go outside and look up into the sky. As a child, I somehow felt safer that Dad was outside "protecting us," so I guess I think that I'm protecting my family. Charlotte, on the other hand, has been tracking the possibility of this storm since it left Sri Lanka, and has prepared our "hidey hole" hours in advance.

I remember our college days when only one guy on our dorm floor ever went to breakfast. When he returned from the cafeteria, he would give us his weather report as only an All-Conference Defensive End could report, "No cold." That's really all we needed to know. If his clothes were wet, it was raining. If it was cold, he didn't say a word, he just reached in his closet and grabbed a coat. He was our 1968 version of a weather app, and he was always accurate.

Charlotte understands things like high pressure and low-pressure systems, barometric pressure, heat index, and she can point out the "hook" in the approaching severe thunderstorm. I have never been able to identify the "hook;" I just know that green means rain, and red means lots of rain. Charlotte will point to a bunch of lines on her phone app and say, "Do you see that wind?" I will quickly glance out the window, see the leaves blowing, and with my most concerned voice say, "Yep, wind's blowing."

I know that a lot of people need to closely watch the weather because of their occupations, but for Charlotte it is more of an obsession. I'm not saying that's terrible; I'm just saying we're different. When I walk outside with our dog in the morning, we stroll for a few minutes until he's ready to go back inside. When we walk through the door, my weather-watching wife will always say, "Is it cloudy?" Then, and only then, it dawns on me that I never even thought to look up at the sky. Normally, my response will be, "Not bad."

I'm just saying that, unlike my wife, I'm just not into weather, but come rain or shine, "This is the day that the Lord has made", and we will, "rejoice and be glad in it."

I sure hope those Jupiteranians have found a "hidey hole."

Chapter 35

A Thanksgiving Lesson

Our son, Kyle, left Mississippi the Monday morning before Thanksgiving, headed for Arkansas with his famous smoked turkey in the back seat of a 2019 popular model car. The car had been checked out and a recently issued recall had been repaired. No need to put the turkey in a cooler. It was one of 250 that he and his friend had smoked all night to feed the employees at a hospital. Grab a turkey, jump in the recently repaired car, and surprise mom and dad by arriving earlier than expected. What could go wrong? Well, you obviously don't know our family.

While driving happily over a Southeast Arkansas road, the car sputtered, stalled, stopped, and died. Kyle was able to get it off the highway and onto a side road. He called his insurance guy, roadside assistance, and then called us. After making sure that he was okay, I asked the important question, "Do I need to come and rescue that smoked turkey?" Kyle assured me that the tow truck was on the way, that they would be towing the car to Little Rock, and that I could pick him and the turkey up in a couple of hours.

Two hours later he called to say that the tow truck was just now leaving Little Rock. "Don't worry about the turkey," he reassured me. As it turns out, a nice man who lived close by came to check on Kyle, and provided the right combination of ice and plastic bags for the turkey. He first had looked for one of his many ice chests, but it's deer season in Arkansas, so all his ice chests were on loan to family members. He even loaded Kyle and the turkey into his truck for a quick ride to a local gas station to purchase a cooler, but as already stated, it's deer season in Arkansas. There were no coolers. Anyway, the ice and plastic bags worked perfectly.

He also provided much-needed conversation to help Kyle's four-hour wait pass by more quickly. Kyle thanked him and asked what he could do to repay him for his kindness. The man said, "There is one thing you can do for me. You can pray for me." Kyle said, "I can do that, in fact, I can do that right now." The nice man explained that he had struggled for a long time with an addiction, but he had been clean for a while, and had even regained custody of his children. "But," he said, "things are hard right now." So, on the side of the road, Kyle prayed for his new friend who then said, "The opportunity to do something nice for someone and that prayer will get me through the day."

Selfishly, as I reflected on that story, I was thankful that the recently repaired car broke down near the house of a kind man who took care of my son and that delicious turkey. Both arrived safely. However, as we reflected more, we realized that God's ultimate purpose for the car breaking down when and where it did had nothing to do with us, but with a man who was struggling and needed an opportunity to be blessed and to be a blessing. In that exact moment, he needed someone to pray for him.

I'm just saying that it's not always about us turkeys, but about the many along the highways who need a personal contact, and a prayer. "It's not about me," is one of life's most important lessons.

Chapter 36

An Unforgettable Christmas

I don't even remember which Christmas song was playing as I was driving up the road to our house. It was that time of day, twilight, when nostalgia suddenly seems to invade my mind and stir my emotions. In an instant, it was Christmas, and I was eight years old, sitting on my dad's footstool in front of a cedar Christmas tree, which was covered with multicolored lights and shiny tinsel. Tears came, and with them a deep longing in my heart for a time long ago when warmth from our kitchen would flow into the small living room and warm a boy's heart. There was such contentment there.

Twilight has always been my favorite time of day, but now that I'm in my twilight years, that time of day brings on an acute nostalgia. It seems strange that I would think more about my parents now than I did when they were on earth. I can instantly mind-travel to our home just outside of Hope and see my mother standing in the kitchen and see my dad working in his garden. Sights, sounds, and smells are vivid and real, and then the tears flow … especially at Christmastime.

There is one unforgettable Christmas morning that always comes to mind. On that very early Christmas morning, Dad and I were driving into town. I hesitate to tell you why we were going into town so early because then I will have to confess that we always opened presents days before Christmas. It would start with one of us saying, "Let's just open one present apiece after supper." We would repeat that night after night until the only thing left under the tree on Christmas morning was the tree stand. So, you're thinking, "What was there to look forward to on Christmas morning?" Well, Dad and I would get up early, go to my cousins' house and watch them open their Christmas presents. I always looked forward to seeing what Joe, Tom, and Brenda were getting for Christmas. It was a weird family tradition, but I loved being with my cousins on Christmas morning.

So, on that very early Christmas morning, Dad and I were driving into town. The streetlights were still shining brightly, gas lights at the end of sidewalks were still lit, a few houses showed signs of activity, and there was a heavy, heavy fog. It was such a strange sight with the lights attempting to break through the thick fog. The dim lights shining through the fog truly looked like stars that had temporarily fallen to earth. In a way it was a little scary. My dad slowed the car down and almost came to a complete stop, and then he said, "I've never seen anything like this. It's like Jesus may be coming."

I've never forgotten that strangely beautiful sight on that early Christmas morning, and I still remember the wonder and excitement in Dad's voice when he said, "It's like Jesus may be coming."

I'm just saying that Jesus is coming, and I believe it will be soon. It would be fitting for Him to return on the day set apart for celebrating His birth, but whichever day He chooses, it will be like nothing we have ever seen. Amen. Come, Lord Jesus.

Chapter 37

What It's Really All About

"That's what it's all about." Those are the words spoken by Coach Nick Saban right after Alabama had defeated Cincinnati to move on to the Finals of the College Football Championship. Interestingly, I heard the same comment in the parking lot at Walmart just a few weeks ago. Two guys were talking about the recent retirement of a mutual friend and one of the guys said, "He retired, sold their house, and bought a house on the lake. That's what it's all about."

I wish I had kept a list of how many times I have heard, "That's what it's all about," and the many different situations to which those words were applied. I may have even said those words during the holidays when our entire family, all 15 of us, gathered on Christmas Eve. What is it really all about? It certainly can't be the Hokey Pokey! What does this often-used statement even mean?

I tend to over analyze at times, but what is the "it" that it's all about? If winning a football game, moving to a house on the lake, celebrating the birth of Christ with family, sitting in front of a warm fire with a cup of coffee, holding a newborn baby, or watching a sunset on a picturesque lake can all be "what it's all about," then what is the definition of "it?" Is "it" a recognition of accomplishment, a sense of peace, a state of contentment, an overflow of joy, or a serenity that is overwhelmingly calming? Is "it" any of that? Is "it" all of that?

Whatever "it" is, it's a big deal because it's what everything (all) is about. So, "it" cannot be something that comes and goes with changing emotions, or goes away when the fire dies down, or the coffee gets cold, or the darkness appears after the sunset. What is there that is what everything is all about, all the time?

Whatever "it" is, it must be greater than the physical, greater than the emotional, and greater than the sensual. So, it must be spiritual. In my opinion, "it" is the assurance that I am at peace with God, and I am at peace with His purpose for my life. That, it seems to me, is what "it" is all about.

I have officiated enough funerals to observe that, at the end of the day, what matters most is not how many championships have been won, or where our houses were located, or what kind of inheritance we have left behind, but what your family and friends will need and want is the assurance of your eternal salvation, and the assurance that you are safe in the loving arms of God. I assure you that for your family, that will be "what it's all about."

I'm just saying that it is not too late to find peace with God through faith in Jesus, and realize the purpose for which you were created. That, my friend, is what it's all about.

Chapter 38
The Complete Adequacy of God

"How do I deliver the mail when my best friend just died?" The retired rural letter carrier answered from experience, "You just do what you have to do."

Interestingly, I found the above paragraph in a church newsletter written on December 26, 1991. It was part of a very nice article about my dad, who had gone to Heaven just one week earlier. Upon hearing about Dad's death, his longtime friend and local mailman knocked on the door of a mutual friend and co-worker, and asked him this thought-provoking question, "How do I deliver the mail when my best friend just died?" The veteran mailman's reply is just as thought- provoking, "You just do what you have to do." Since reading that paragraph, I cannot get that early morning conversation out of my mind.

Most of us have found ourselves in similar situations. Tragedy strikes and our immediate response is, "How?" How am I going to take the next step, make the next decision, or face the next day? Comfort does not come easily. As family and friends surround us, we know their words are true, but they seem jumbled. Just today as I was listening to a Christian radio station, two songs were accidentally being played at the same time. I knew the words of both songs and they are beautiful words, but their true meaning was so distorted and so jumbled that they lost their intended impact. Such are most well-meaning words in times of debilitating grief or emotional trauma.

I understand the retired rural letter carrier's response, "You just do what you have to do." There's certainly truth in that counsel. I remember being told many times by my coaches to, "Hold your head up!" Translated that means, "Do not become so discouraged or so overwhelmed that you lose your desire to fight the good fight, to finish the course, to keep the faith."

Yes, the mail has to be delivered. Life has to move on, the next steps have to be taken, decisions have to be made, but how we choose to respond in those moments is crucial. God does not abandon us to survive on our own. The greatest blessing that comes out of grief, sorrow, and heartbreak is the discovery of the adequacy of God. He will give you both the desire and the strength to move on. He will comfort, heal, encourage, strengthen, love, and provide whatever is needed when it is most needed. He will carry the mail.

I'm just saying that realizing our inadequacy is the first step in discovering the complete adequacy of God. Keep your head up ... way up ... always looking to the One who loves you most.

"Trust in the Lord with all your heart And do not lean on your own understanding. In all your ways acknowledge Him, And He will make your paths straight." (Proverbs 3:5-6 NASB)

Chapter 39

Laughing at Ourselves

I preached my first sermon on Mother's Day in 1974, forty-eight years ago. After much prayer and very little study, I was able to come up with enough material to challenge the folks at Bluff Springs Missionary Baptist Church for seven minutes. It was the most underwhelming seven minutes of my ministry, but my mother said it was the best Mother's Day ever.

Like many of you, I will be thinking about my mother this Sunday. Betty Lou Ellis Parris has been in Heaven since 1984, and I still miss her. I have written about her a lot, especially in my book, *Just Outside of Hope*, but there are a few memories that just the two of us shared for a long time ... she swore me to secrecy.

I was about 13 years old, and Mother and I were at home alone when one of those cold, winter storms left us without electricity. My dad must have been at a church meeting or a Masonic Lodge meeting because he was rarely away from home after dark. Mother had the gas wall heaters burning, so we were warm, but in the dark except for the kerosene lamp.

There were no heaters in either of the two bedrooms, so when bedtime came, Mother grabbed the flashlight and held it as I crawled underneath the bed to plug in the electric blanket. It dawned on both of us at the exact same time that the electric blanket would not provide much warmth without electricity. Mother was laughing so hard that she sat down on the floor, turned off the flashlight and left me stranded and laughing under my bed. I don't remember the two of us ever laughing together like that. Today, thinking about that laughter brings tears to my eyes.

Mother was one of the hardest workers I've ever known. She worked for 33 years at a sewing factory, sitting at a sewing machine eight hours a day. Mother never learned to drive, so after work she rode with other ladies who would drop her off at Longs Grocery Store about 100 yards from our house. She would often go into the store to buy milk, bread, and something she might need to cook for supper.

On this particular hot, summer day, she had walked up the dusty road after a long day of sewing heavy winter coats in a building with no air conditioning. She was carrying a sack of groceries in each arm when she arrived at the door and realized that she did not have her key. She set the grocery sacks down on the doorstep and walked to the back of the house to an unlocked bedroom window. In those days, we always left a back window unlocked just in case we forgot the key. Go ahead and laugh, but the strategy worked that day, and my tired mother climbed through that window in her dress, walked through the house, unlocked the door, and then climbed right back out of that back window, walked back to the front door, picked up those groceries and entered the house through the unlocked door. She told me that she did not realize what she had just done until she set the groceries down on the kitchen table.

When she told me that story through outbursts of laughter, she made me promise not to tell Dad, and I never did, but I know that sometime later she confessed. After that experience, we always left a door key in a not very well-hidden hiding place. Times were different.

One of the reasons I share that story is that it clearly describes two things that I hold dear about the memory of my mother. She worked hard for her family, sometimes to the point of exhaustion. Now that I'm older, I can better understand that kind of distraction at the end of a long day, but even then I knew without asking that on that hot, summer day, Mother was focused on what she was going to prepare for supper. She took pride in her country cooking, and in her mind, as she crawled in and out of that back window, she could already smell the cornbread and hear the pressure cooker getting the butter beans just right. She went to great lengths to take care of us.

I'm just saying that sharing laughter, especially laughing at ourselves, is one of the first memories that pops into my mind as I remember my mother. I would love to hear her laugh once more.

Chapter 40

Making Every Second Count

"The clock is ticking." At the time of writing these words, it has clicked approximately 2 billion times since I was born at 5:45 p.m. on May 30, 1949. I have paid attention to ticking clocks for most of my life. I remember watching those large wall clocks in the classrooms of Hope High School and thinking, in some classes, that 50 minutes seemed like a lifetime. Ticking clocks were important during basketball games, and football games. In track, even half ticks could make a difference. I remember a few "buzzer beaters" when one more tick would have changed the record books.

My dad always said that as you got older, the clock would tick faster. That made absolutely no sense to an 18-year-old, but today the ticks are not only faster, but louder. In fact, at times they are deafening. I also remember my dad saying, when he was about the age I am today, that he spent a lot of time going to funerals. Once again, he was right. Of course, attending funerals has been part of my 48 years in the ministry, but only recently have I noticed that at most funerals I'm one of the oldest persons in the room. That fact has become true at all events, not just funerals.

A ticking clock is just part of life and a solemn reminder that every clock will have a final tick. Every clock will run out of time. We don't even know how much time is left on the clock, but we do know that there will be a final tick. So, every tick counts. Life is not like a sporting event where you must play the game while watching the clock, but we should live our lives knowing that there is a clock … and it is ticking. So, having established the fact that I am older than I've ever been, that my clock is ticking faster and louder than it ever has, and that I have fewer ticks left today than I did yesterday, what does it all mean?

For me, as a Christ follower, it means I'm closer to Heaven than I've ever been, and I am smiling when I say that. I believe that we are eternal beings, and that we will live forever somewhere. What we refer to as "death" is just the doorkeeper into eternity. Because of my trust in Jesus, and in Him alone, my eternity will be in His presence. Big smile.

It also means that I desire to finish strong. I want my last ticks to be productive in His Kingdom, but honestly, that is becoming a greater challenge than it should be. For one thing, as the ticks go faster, I seem to go slower. It takes me longer to get things ticking. However, I am thankful for those whom God placed in my life to teach me how to walk (not run) in the Spirit, therefore, it does not matter how fast the clock is ticking, but rather, what does matter is that I am walking closely with God, that I am controlled by His Spirit, and that I am available at every tick to be used by Him and for His glory.

Those who know me best, know that I am a counter. I count things … like ceiling tiles in the doctor's office, the number of steps to the mailbox, the number of attendees at the tree lighting ceremony in a Hallmark movie, the number of pews in a church, the number of French fries in a McDonald's order, and … well, you get the picture. When I was playing football, I always lined up eleven yards off the ball, so I measure everything in 11-yard increments. I just enjoy counting; it is relaxing and comforting to me. So, I am not only old, but strangely weird.

Psalm 90:12 says, "*So teach us to number our days, That we may present to You a heart of wisdom.*" We do not know how many days, much less how many ticks, but we know that we will stand before a righteous God and present to him an accounting of what we've done with those ticks.

Chapter 41

Choosing Heroes

Well, I attended another funeral today. It was in my hometown of Hope, Arkansas, and unlike most events that I have recently attended, I was not the oldest person in the room. In fact, I may have been among the youngest.

As I looked around the room, I mind-traveled back to the early 1960s, my junior high school years. The man whose life we were celebrating was one of my heroes as a seventh and eighth grader. He was a superb high school athlete as a young man, and, in adulthood, became the quality individual you want your heroes to be. It was obvious by the packed church sanctuary that many people still have great respect and admiration for kind, gracious, family-oriented men who love God. David Porterfield was exactly that kind of man.

There was also an unspoken, yet obvious, understanding among all present that we were not just mourning the loss of a friend, but also we were face to face with the loss of an era … our era. That's not to say that the world is immediately coming to an end, but the world that we grew up in, the world full of our young memories and our young heroes, is hanging by a thread.

As we began the memorial service, it was not sadness that was squeezing my heart and bringing tears to my eyes, but rather, it was gratitude. Gratitude that I had shared a hometown, a high school, a tradition, as well as many youthful memories with people like these. But we were no longer youth, and now we all had much more in common. As one of the speakers said, "We are now in the fourth quarter, and for some of us it's "overtime."

When we stood to sing, my first thought was that we should sing our old high school alma mater, but then, we begin to sing what could be our new alma mater:

A mighty fortress is our God,
a bulwark never failing;
our helper he, amid the flood
of mortal ills prevailing.

For still our ancient foe
does seek to work us woe;
his craft and power are great,
and armed with cruel hate,
on earth is not his equal.

Did we in our own strength confide,
our striving would be losing,
were not the right Man on our side,
the Man of God's own choosing.

You ask who that may be?
Christ Jesus, it is he;
Lord Sabaoth his name,
from age to age the same;
and he must win the battle.

It was a perfect song for older people to stand and sing together. We seem to stand taller with each verse, and suddenly we were sharing more than a hometown, more than a tradition, and more than youthful memories … we were sharing Biblical hope.

The man we were celebrating was a committed follower of Christ. In fact, in his mid-fifties he followed the leading of the Lord into vocational ministry. His departure from this life was unexpected and sudden. He passed from this life into eternal life on a Sunday morning. Fitting.

Most of us stayed and visited for a moment after the service. We relived some of those old memories, like his 57-yard touchdown to beat Nashville, although some now say it was a 75-yard touchdown. We talked most about his adult life, and how in his quiet, steady manner he had impacted so many. The last words of our new alma mater were fresh on our minds:

> Let goods and kindred go,
> this mortal life also;
> the body they may kill:
> God's truth abideth still;
> His kingdom is forever!

I'm just saying that, as a young teen, I did a good job picking heroes.

Chapter 42

Our Stability

One of the joys of being a Christian is hearing God speak to my spirit as I read the Bible. I wholeheartedly believe that God communicates with us through His divinely inspired written Word. It might be a chapter, a verse, a phrase, or just one word that prompts my spirit in a way that says, "Pay attention, read it again, and hear what I am saying to you."

Recently, as I was reading in Isaiah, this verse captured my attention: *"And He will be the stability of your times, A wealth of salvation, wisdom and knowledge; The fear of the Lord is his treasure."*

I was fairly certain that I understood the meaning of the word "stability," but just to be sure, I double-checked, and my definition was correct: *Not likely to give way or overturn; firmly fixed.* It probably will not surprise you to know that my first lesson about stability was during a seventh grade football practice.

Our Coach explained the principles of the three-point stance while using me as his example. While I was in my stance, he pushed me from behind and I fell forward. I readjusted my stance, he pushed me from the front, and I fell backwards. When he pushed me from the left side, l fell to the right, etc. After several embarrassing attempts, I finally achieved the perfect, stable, stance, and was firmly fixed. He then blew the whistle for me to "fire out of my stance," and well, that speed thing required a lot more coaching.

Stability is necessary for a lot of things.

Stability is necessary to survive strong storms … storms of any kind. If God is your stability, whatever storms are attempting to blow you off of your foundation through discouragement, distress, distraction, or depression will not succeed. God promises to "be the stability" of anytime every time.

Certainly the "times" in which we are living could stand some stability. Could it be that the reason most things (and some people) are so unstable, so seemingly about "to give way and overturn," is because we are not "firmly fixed?" Admitting that obvious truth is the first step that must be taken.

Stability is a result of having the right foundation. When you look closely at this verse in Isaiah and see that God is a wealth of salvation, a wealth of wisdom, and a wealth of knowledge, it really makes you wonder why we would ever be so foolish to reject being firmly fixed on Him. The reason for our foolishness is revealed in that final phrase, *The fear of the Lord is his treasure.*

Stability can only be realized when it has been built on reverence and respect for God … the one, true, living and righteous God. The current winds of modern "times" not only do not recognize the fear of the Lord as a "treasure," they seem to be attempting to "blow it off," and blow it out of our culture completely. No wonder there is such an absence of wisdom, and "sanctified common sense" (a phrase I use to describe my godly parents).

I'm just saying, dear friend, when God is your treasure, you are firmly fixed and are not likely to be blown or pushed over. Your "times" are in His hands.

Chapter 43

Drawing Names

Every year, during Thanksgiving, our family has a tradition of drawing names for Christmas gifts. On Thanksgiving Day, fifteen names will be written on individual slips of paper, placed into a Chicago Cubs World Series Champions baseball cap, and passed around the room. The fun begins as we watch the expression on each person's face as they see whose name they have picked. Of course, all names are to be kept secret until gifts are exchanged on Christmas Eve, but we have a few family members who immediately begin to try to piece the puzzle together and figure out who has whose name.

A few years ago, Charlotte and I thought it would be fun to write my name on each slip of paper and watch the reactions. The joke kind of backfired as each person pulled my name out of the hat, shook their head from side-to-side, and either breathed a sigh of disappointment or breathed out loud, "Oh, no." Apparently, no one in the family wants to draw my name because I am "so hard to shop for." Comments each year include, "Dad never wants anything," or "Papa will never tell us what he wants." For the most part, they are right.

As a boy, the most important Christmas gift I received every year was new underwear and new T-shirts ... six of each to be exact. My mother made sure that my supply of underwear was updated and that I always had a drawer full of "nice" underwear "in case I had to go to the hospital." She was very serious about that. Charlotte and I bought Mother a very nice bathrobe one year as a Christmas gift, and she said that "it was too nice to wear," and that she was "going to save it and wear it if I have to go to the hospital."

So, this Thanksgiving Day when the names are drawn out of the hat, I will immediately know who has the unfortunate task of choosing something to give me for Christmas. Their head will drop, there will be an obvious sigh, and everyone in the room will know who drew Papa's name. Later, that unfortunate family member will contact Charlotte and ask, "What can I get him, does he need anything, does he want anything?" Charlotte will say, "I have no idea, I've already bought his underwear."

Honestly, everything I need and want will be gathered in our living room on Thanksgiving Day. The names in that baseball cap mean the world to me. I need them to know how much I love them. I need them to know that family is, and will always be, important. I need them to want to carry on these family gatherings even when my name is no longer in the hat. I want them to find, follow, and fulfill God's will for their lives. I need them to understand how important that is to me.

I'm just saying that I want the person who draws my name to know that what I really want is a new Chicago Cubs World Series Champions baseball cap. No pressure.

Chapter 44

New "Homeowner"

"Helping cats feel at home" says the cat food commercial. Sure. We now share our home with a nine-month-old Calico female beast. Not only does she "feel at home," she believes that she is now the homeowner.

A little history for clarification: I am not really a cat person. While living in Venezuela, we had a cat, Leonela, for the purpose of decreasing the iguana population that hung in the trees around our house. It's not that we disliked iguanas, but iguanas are vegetarians and they poop a lot. Running from the car to the front door without being hit became an all-to-frequent challenge, thus the cat. Leonela was a great hunter, even going up into the trees after the iguanas, but she also had a gestation period of about 24 hours. We soon had generations of cats, and we decided that the iguana problem was not as serious as we had first believed.

Anyway, last summer, I asked our 16-year-old granddaughter, Sara, to go with me to get some home-grown tomatoes at a friend's farm. If I had known that our friend's barn was full of kittens, I would never have taken Sara. You know the rest of the story ... we came home with some beautiful, delicious tomatoes and a wild, barn kitten.

Arriving home, our new pet immediately bit Charlotte's finger to the bone, requiring a week of antibiotics and a tetanus shot. "Helping cats feel at home" was the last thing on my mind for the first several months of sharing our home with this cat. We are dog people. We are adjusting. Cats are not dogs. I cannot emphasize that enough.

We experimented with a few names for our cat, but none seemed to really catch her demeanor and personality. I suggested a Spanish name, which is translated windy or gassy, but has a different slang meaning in Venezuela. Obviously, our cat understands Spanish slang and was greatly offended by the name. She hates me.

The only toy she will play with is a small stuffed dog. She swats it, bites it, actually throws it into the air and catches it with her feet while glancing our way as if to say, "Take that, dog people." She thinks my hands are toys to be attacked. She perches on the back of my chair, watching birds through the window while swinging her puffed-up tail across my face like a windshield wiper.

Even though she has a nice, expensive scratching post, she is demolishing the back of my chair.

She gallops through the house at full speed like a horse. Our vet says that all kittens have endorphins that create these outbursts of energy, but when I'm watching this, all I can think about is when Jesus cast the demons into the swine and they rambled head-first off the cliff. Just saying.

I must admit that she is an amazingly athletic creature. The only things in our house that she has not climbed are the refrigerator and the hutch. She is able to walk across a table full of breakable items without touching them. Her quickness is remarkable. Her cleanliness is admirable. She alerts us when it's time to clean the litter box by standing in front of it and making a strange, guttural cry. It sounds like an opera soprano attempting to clear phlegm from her throat. It's more than a little scary.

She will occasionally sit in Charlotte's lap … when she wants to. She will occasionally snuggle with Sara … when she wants to.

She will run at full speed, leap onto my chair with my very visible body sitting in it, and make her way to her favorite perch. The only part of me she ever acknowledges are my hands which, in her mind, are like gazelles to a stalking lion. It is very difficult to take a nap in my chair with my hands in my pockets. As I said, we are adjusting.

She sleeps 16-18 hours a day somewhere in our house. We can never find her when we want to, but rattle the cat food bag and she will immediately and strangely just appear. No sound, no warning, she just appears, standing right behind us. She loves her cat food, but ignores her water bowl, choosing rather to drink from the toilet and unroll about five yards of toilet paper.

She seems to "feel at home," but I don't think she has yet decided if she will allow us to stay. However, Sara loves her and I think, in time, after she has destroyed my chair and scratched all flesh from my hands, that I will be able to forgive my friends for inviting me to come pick up some of their beautiful, delicious, home-grown tomatoes. Just saying.

About the Author

The Rev. Stan Parris, an author, former pastor, missions pastor, and missionary, has written a second book after considerable success with his first title, *Just Outside of Hope*, a book about how the Lord led him on mission journeys throughout the world, including a residential missionary post in Maracaibo, Venezuela.

Stan retired as pastor of Second Baptist Church in Arkadelphia, Arkansas, a small town that is home to two universities—Henderson State University, a public school, and Ouachita Baptist University, a private Southern Baptist University that supplies more denominational preachers and music ministers than any school in Arkansas. Stan graduated from Henderson, which is a small part of the unusual path of his life from "just outside of Hope," Arkansas, where he grew up, to All-America college football player, to an NFL camp where he was one misstep from making the team, to coaching high school football, then surrendering to his long-held call to the ministry, which led to a call to missions.

He graduated from Southwestern Baptist Theological Seminary in Fort Worth, Texas, then pastored churches in Arizona, Oklahoma, and Arkansas, became missions pastor at one of the largest Southern Baptist Churches in his home state, eventually ending his fulltime ministry in the town where and when football was No. 1 in his life. His priorities changed, both with his marriage and his call to the ministry. His love of preaching has not diminished in retirement, leading him to interim pastorships and opportunities to fill in for pastors on leave or vacation.

Stan married his college sweetheart, Charlotte Wilson Parris, and they have three children, Kyle, Kelly, and Kenneth. Stan and Charlotte also are "Papa" and "Nana" to five grandchildren—Alexa Nicole, Dustyn James, Sara Elizabeth, Charlee Lane, and Campbell Elise. The newest addition to the family is great-grandson, Beckham James Spinks.

Printed in the USA
CPSIA information can be obtained
at www.ICGtesting.com
CBHW020434271023
1530CB00001B/2